CLASSIFICATION: POETRY

This book is sold under the condition that it shall
not, by way of trade or otherwise, be lent, resold,
hired out or otherwise circulated without the pub-
lisher's prior consent in any form of binding or cover
other than that in which it is published and without
a similar condition including this condition being
imposed on the subsequent purchaser.

A CIP catalogue record for this book is available
from the British Library.

Printed and bound in Great Britain.

*Cover photograph by courtesy of
the Yorkshire Tourist Board.*

This Scotland, Northern Ireland and Isle of Man edition

ISBN 1-902803-98-1

First published in Great Britain in 2001 by
United Press Ltd
44a St James Street
Burnley
BB11 1NQ
Tel: 01282 459533
Fax: 01282 412679
ISBN for complete set of volumes
1-902803-99-X
All Rights Reserved

www.upltd.co.uk

Visions
in
Verse

Foreword

In my humble opinion the old saying that all things come to those who wait is utter balderdash. I've always believed that you have got to make the effort if you are going to succeed. The poets who feature in this compilation all have that excellent and admirable quality in abundance. They have all made a great personal effort to express themselves, to communicate, and to show that they have confidence in their talent.

That's why I'm so pleased that we at United Press could give these poets a platform upon which to showcase their gift for putting their thoughts into words. Publication in a compilation like this can be, for so many, a major step forward as a writer. It gives encouragement to new poets, fresh hope to experienced ones, and joy to all.

Peter Quinn, Editor

Contents

The poets who have contributed to this volume are listed below, along with the relevant page upon which their work can be found.

60	John Fraser Hynd	89	Louise Latto
	Sheila MacFarlane	90	Robbie Innes
61	Lucy McManus	91	Brenda Jane Williams
	Elaine Donaldson	92	Sue Ellis
62	Samantha Osborne	93	Faye Richardson
63	Carol Seivewright	94	Rachel Bodell
64	John MacDonald	95	Glenys Penman
65	Eleanor Hamilton	96	William Hamilton
66	Alexander Cuthbert	97	Alexander Mackay
67	Anna Mathers	98	Mairead Macbeath
	Margaret C Rae	99	April Uprichard
68	Jane Thomson	100	Ann Hogarth
	Sheila MacMillan	101	Leigh Stewart
69	Ra Sefako	102	Jonathan Finlay
70	Catherine Seiler	103	Madeline McCully
	M Hardman	104	Joy Bell
71	Karen O'Neill	105	Betty Devenney
72	Alison Tavendale	106	Gemma Walker
73	Jennifer Brown	107	Linda Callaghan
	Mary Gemmell	108	Aisling Doherty
74	Helen Dick		Linda Smith
	Montgomery Lindsay	109	Beatrice M Wilson
75	Helen Osborne	110	Elaine Warren French
76	Jacqui Hogan	111	John V McManus
	Sandra MacLean	112	Caroline Morton
77	Victoria Young	113	Simon Maltman
	Laura McLeod		Nancy Callow
78	Maisie Miller	114	Noel Lindsay
79	Jean Lunan		Matthew Walker
	Chris Clancey	115	Shelley Tracey
80	Kay Clements	116	Adrian McGinley
	Robin Drew	117	Julieann Campbell
81	Andrew Lamb	118	Joanne Peden
82	Amritash Agrawalla		John Deehan
83	Denise Gildea	119	Marlene McKenzie
84	Wilma Barty	120	Pearse Coyle
	Naomi Howarth	121	Damian Begley
85	D S Anderson		Suzanne McCrory
86	Alyson Hunter	122	Louise McMonagle
	Sara Jane Duffus	123	Sheila Jameson
87	Ian Fowler	124	Sadie Higgins
88	Lorna Sim	125	Lynne Morrow

126	E M Gillen
127	M A McCafferty
128	Victor Shaw
	Alan Lawton
129	Patricia O'Reilly
130	Aaron Donaghy
131	Colette Timony
132	Maeve Cairns
133	A Belshaw
134	John Coups
135	Victor McMullen
	Louise Gibson
136	Edel Jordan
	Wilma Lewsley
137	Mrs M Smith
138	Hugh Harley
139	Mrs R Dornan
	Robert Gillespie
140	Brigidette McAnea
141	Lisa Doherty
142	Lucinda McCloskey
143	Nuala McKay
144	Noel Spence
145	Natalie Dunn
146	Norah Burnett
147	Clare Rainey
148	Tessa Johnston
149	Jemma Robinson
	Colin Dardis
150	John F McCartney
151	Patricia Miller
152	Maureen J Archbold
153	Cathy Kelly
154	Jean Gardner
155	Derek Keilty
156	Ivan Walton
157	Hazel Wilson

ST VALENTINE'S SPRAY

This card was meant for you dear Mol,
Your lover's verses would enthral,
He'd planned to keep you teased, surprised,
Your card's delivery personalized,
But happenings on the ether written,
Decreed your happy meeting smitten.
To rendezvous, your guy was lured
By thugs, to murderous deeds inured,
Instead of deals and fine bonhomie's,
Came bullets sprayed by noisy "tommys",
No loving hearts do here entwine
on this day of St Valentine,
If to us, "Val" did call to visit,
He'd say, "This ain't your day Mol - is it?"

Alexander Jamieson, Ayrshire

Alexander Jamieson said: My above poem is one of the
four hundred and fifty poems, ballads and limericks etc I've
written and published, the inspiration for which was one
local poem I'd read whilst a recovering car-crash-injured
musician. Years later it dawned on me that music alone
was an insufficient vehicle for human expression, it had to
be my poetry too. Be it terse or tender, comic or cryptic, it
is a statement by me for posterity of my life's experience as
a thinker, mystery - investigation, reader, walker, believer,
humourist, environmentalist. It's all encapsulatde in the
latest collection of poems I have published 'Strange but
New' available at £4.95 (plus £1 P&P) per copy from:
Alexander Jamieson, 28 Cochrane Street, Kilbirnie,
Ayrshire, KA25 7AS.

OVER-CONSUMPTION

Ordinary consumers in the main,
Come snow or sunshine wind or rain,
Expect to go on getting better off,
So does the toff, graspingly for money.

But what now is money, still something real,
Or something funny, virtual, without feel?
Not coin nor paper, fit only for the raper,
The globalist seeking to control; some caper.

Barter is no more - money rules. Some see it other.
Are they merely fools, but globalists tools?
What is our hope, what is our portion?
Are all our lives but money's abortion.

Perhaps, maybe, the globalists will become more gentle,
Kinder, and our world will smile, be free of guile,
Filled with global light from morn till night.
To the banishment of fright - so goodnight my children.

My children bright, sleep, dream, play on, grow tall
till over-consumption turns out the light,
For us all.

Kenneth Holland, Argyll

Dedicated to my Mother and Father who both worked and suffered harder for less than I have.

Born in Stoke **Ken Holland**, enjoys hill walking and antiquarian interests. "I write poetry to keep my brain alive during retirement and to keep in touch with my daughter who is also a writer," explained Kenneth. "My style is off-the-cuff-catholic. I would like to be remembered as an ordinary fellow who trod quietly through his very varied life." Aged 81 Ken is retired with an ambition to help fight the battle against drugs. He is married to Betty and they have 2 children. "I have written over 50 poems but this is only the second which I have had published although I've written alot of correspondence," he said, "My biggest nightmare is being stuck under ground in a dark, wet, cave."

ANGEL

bovine perhaps, not pretty you'd say
with narrow lips and a long nose
but the eyes portray from deep within
the beauty of an angel
caring and compassionate
truthful, kind and giving
those around whom she befriends
are the richer for her living

Sheila Fraser, Angus

WHEN I GO CAMPING

When I go camping,
I have to have sausages for breakfast.

When I go camping,
I have to climb the tallest mountain there.

When I go camping,
I can never build up my tent.

I sometimes get the feeling,

I DON'T LIKE CAMPING.

Laura Hogg, Dundee

*I'd like to dedicate my poem to my gran, Wallace, because
she is so patient and kind and never gets angry.*

CHANCE MEETING

She was beautiful and tall,
Long dark hair.
I met her on a beach,
Worshipping from afar,
On a distant shore of an island,
Which I don't know the name of.
My behaviour seems erratic,
Unpredictable,
Hard to focus.
But we meet, Smile,
Share a lifetime worth of smiles.
In one day.
She was the love of my life.
Who would have thought?
She dies the next day
And I wake up.
Relief
And regret.

Chris Watt, Peterhead

Chris Watt is a keen film and writing enthusiast. "I started writing plays at the age of 15 and from there went the next step to screenwriting," he explained. "I have only started writing poems recently. I am strongly influenced by the writing of Bob Dylan and William Shakespeare. My style is expressionist and surreal and I would like to be remembered as someone who told a good story that made people laugh, cry or feel something new." Aged 21 he is a freelance writer with an ambition to be a professional screenwriter as well as director of his own work. He is single and the person he would most like to meet is Bob Dylan. "His writing is some of the most influential poetry I have ever heard," added Chris.

THE WIDOW

The house is very still. Like me it lies
drained of delight and shrouded in its pain.

You are away... and I alone must go
up empty stairs and into lonely rooms
which yield to me their aching sympathy.

I hear them say, 'We too are listless, lost,
because he is not here. We know your grief
and all your grief's despair. We too have been
invaded, changed forever, and bereft...'

Fading, the voices whisper,
'What is left?'

May C MacKay, Insch

GYROSCOPE

Wheels within wheels.
A blur of rotation
In perfect balance.

The movements of planets
Harnessed in a glittering,
Earthbound instrument,
Of beautiful precision.

The delicate accuracy,
Of artistic engineering,
Pointing the way,
To the stars.

Roger Barnett, Aberdeen

THE EARTH STRIKES BACK

It isn't fair that we pollute the air
The way we throw away our rubbish without a care
What once was white, now turns black
And we wonder why the earth strikes back

She sends a tidal wave to seek revenge
With help from mother nature and all her friends
A tornado sends havoc, the strong winds blow
A volcano brings a river of molten glow.

Where will she strike next, no one knows
A sudden earthquake to keep you on your toes
The ground will shake, the rivers rise
Bringing floods up to your eyes

We inject our poison into the earth veins
Dumping waste and leaving stains
It's not to late we can still save
Before we send each other to our grave

Clean up our lives, clean up this mess
Put ourselves to the test
Working together, stay on track
For we know that the earth strikes back.

Jason Ironside, Peterhead

THE CROCUS

Hermaphrodite incarnate,
Uncrowned head of flowers
Heliotropic trumpet, heralding the sun,
Your variegated leaves, of spear like symetry.
Petals feminine in sunlight, male when day is done.
With my eyes, I gormandize your beauty,
I stand in awe, of your strength, your will to succeed.
As you spring triumphant, from betwixt grass and lowly
weed.

James Goldie, Kilmarnock

FUN IN THE RAIN

Daniel and Connor have new yellow wellies.
Waterproof coats and sou' wester hats.
They run to the biggest puddle to jump in,
Splish-splash! Splish-splash! Puddley-pat!

Two wee Dunoonites who love the rain.
Puddles and drips? Great fun and games.
Laughing, giggling, it's splish-splash fun
For two little cousins both aged one.

Two mucky angels make mud pies
Ready for home? How time flies-
Sou' westers, coats, wellies all black with muck.
Tomorrow they'll go to the pond 'n' feed the hungry ducks.

Two tired toddles now head for home
Each into a warm bath full of foam.
After tea, too weary to fight,
A story in bed, kisses, "Godbless, 'night 'night!"

Patricia Laird, Dunoon

17

TWINS

Twins are fun, twins are trouble
Whatever you need, you need it double
One bike simply just wont do
You'll know you should have bought the two.

Then when you buy them both the same
you've only got yourself to blame.
Fights over ownership apply
you cannot please them if you try.

At bedtime, oh, they do protest
who's hot water bottles best.
At feeding time its like a zoo
One meal will rarely suit the two

With twins you'll always pull out your hair
as one or other won't play fair
but when the fighting's over and done
they'll curl together, melt to one.

When twins are tucked up warm in bed
and Anadin has eased my head
wiggle my toes, and heave a sigh
Give up my twins... I'd rather die.

Bobbi Vetter, Dollar
For Rhiannon and Finn, my bright stars. Love you forever - Mum.

Born in the USA, **Bobbi Vetter** enjoys rehabilitating abused and feral animals. "I started writing bedtime stories for my younger brother Jason and now for my twins," she remarked. "My work is influenced by people and creatures around the farm and my style is untrained and unrestrained." Aged 38 she is an artist with an ambition to undertake the likes of Sistine Chapel. "I live with my partner David children Finn and Rhiannon. The person I would most like to meet is the artist Alan Lee because of his vision in illustrating books. I have written children's poetry and short stories but this is the first time I have had something published."

UNTITLED

What world were with to be, shall in its
truth give credence to the povered such
as we, and ere the day arrive that humble
be, the pulchritude and wisdom will in
your truth forever to be free
oh light oh entheatus tree thy love
in here's the silence of this world begat
in tears and in thy bosom pure and
right give nurture to your truth in
blinding light.

Patrick McBride, Glasgow

THE GREATEST GIFT

The greatest gift
Fate can bestow
No matter what the gender
It makes one's heart to glow
A cuddle is

An arm around you
A moment's balm
From our daily toil and strife
Warmth of another's palm
A cuddle is

To have someone
Embrace you tight
For a moment only you
Turns dark into light
A cuddle is.

Mary Hudson, Helensburgh

THE PSEUDOS

Strident voiced television presenters
Posing as psychiatrists;
So analytical, and critical,
Dabbling with uncertainty,
And prolonging the intolerable,
All, in entertainments name.
'Exploiters' of the vulnerable;
Their privacy now laid bare.

These pseudos then, are clearly here to stay.
When night time comes, does sleep come easily?

Alexander Winter, Aberdeen

ANGELS IN THE DARK

Mystical angles shimmering
On crystal wings
Small rhinestones glimmering
In heavens high a soprano choir sings

Grey stallions cantering studded skies
Saddled steadfastly with peaceful Gods
Silvery stones shine where the crow flies
Slumbering pixies' and elf nods

Spangles of love harnessed on high
Fairies with frosted magic wands
Flickering gems in the twilight
Shooting stars and trailing bands

Ballooning ribbon fringes frail
Into a black sequinned veil.

Ann Copland, Oldmeldrum

A MOTHER'S LOVE

When all around have had their doubts
My mother has shown them what love is all about
She has stood by me through the good times and the bad
Even though most times she's not been happy but sad

I've not been the most perfect ideal son
In fact I've probably been a really horrible one
But to her is hasn't made any difference at all
She was always there to help me when I had a fall

She gives me hope with her undying love
Her strength must come from God in heaven above
To her there is no doubt her silly oldest son
He has a fight and it's going to be won

When I get down and have my moods
She cheers me up as only she could
Her outlook on life, love and anything at all
Make my problems look really pathetic and small

She is the most wonderful person that I know
And every chance I get my love for her I show
There is no one living to match this woman
She's my mother, she's the world most perfect human.

Ian Cullerton, Edinburgh

SONNET 1

Beyond all my heartache,
you slid down the beautiful rainbow's banister
like a child in her home,
straight into my world
of rocks and pebbles.
A tiny little creature if ever I did see,
sitting quietly in the palm of my hand.

I kissed you softly,
multiplying your size as much my heart
until we stood on a level ground
and the rainbow wrapped round your finger.
Then all the songbirds in the garden
sang for me once more
as the flowers in my eyes blossomed again.

Stephen Watt, Dumbarton

Born in Dumbarton, **Stephen Watt** enjoys writing, reading, football, music and jogging. "I started writing poetry when I was 19. I felt my head and heart were ready to burst and poetry was the mess that came out." he explained. "My work is influenced by Carol-Ann Duffy, sunrises and sunsets. I would like to be remembered as an honest and positive poet who cared deeply for those closest to me." Aged 21 he is an office clerk with an ambition to put a smile and glow on everyone's faces and to make a name for himself in the media. One person he would most like to meet is David Gray because of his songwriting abilities. My debut book 'Getting to Know You' was published last year and can be found in the National Library of Britain," he added.

CAN'T BREATH, I'M IN TROUBLE

Under pressure, I'm choking almost run out of gas
The things of the future catch up with the past
Pater is not with us and mater is growing old
She's reaching the end of a life that's well sold
The family is less caring, they've got a life of their own
More interested in themselves than the ancestral home
She's void of an interest, just sits there alone
She cries on occasion but tries not to moan
The business gets done, but, usually mostly by me
The rest should contribute more, the pressure to free
My health has been suffering, my resistance is low
The effects of this huge burden are beginning to show
But as previously mentioned they can't even get into their cars
They've all left the battlefield and collected, no scars
Getting greyer, God I need help from the stresses and strains
I'm grateful, for all the support from the wife and the weans.

Andrew Bryden, Ayr

ONCE I GLANCE

If a single glance can foretell your future
then let me glance once more,
for I need to know more than ever what I was put here for.
Once I glance, twice I do,
but still I know no more than you.
My future it will only be;
when past, and present it becomes,
then all I know.
With just one glance,
let it be,
so I can know all about me.

Mandy Ralston, Kilmarnock

ALL IS ILLUSION

It was told to me, "There is no God."
The world still looked the same.
They said to me, "All is illusion."
The illusion of food tasted good.
I feel I am at home.

I swim in illusions
Like a fish in the water.
I play with illusions
Like a bird in the wind.
I feel I am at home.

Beware of those who shout
To impress their thoughts on others.
To sell an illusion of knowledge.

Bill Waugh, Spean Bridge

MY MAM AND DAD

The pictures of my Mam and Dad
I don't have hanging on the wall
They are forever in my memory
Loving, tender memories to recall

So many years have been and gone
Since they left us for God's call
But my yearning for that childhood
Days, so precious, I would give my soul

But I know there is no turning back
Just forward, onward, go
The memories gathered on the way
I can keep, but to other, never show

Every day that passes, a week, a year
We know not what the future brings
Until suddenly, it's here
Cling to all most precious, all you hold most dear

I must than God for my life on earth
Through good times, and the bad
But the biggest thanks is in my memory
For my lovely Mam and Dad.

Willamina Gibb, Ellon

A CRITICISM OF A POET'S DISCUSSION

I listened to a discussion of poets
On the air
They said that it was difficult
To understand a poets ware

To me a poem is a story
Put into a nutshell
It tells of life, of love and death
In an abbreviated state
And if you can read between the lines
You're never out of date.

James Jardine, Hawick

IT'S ALWAYS DARK

I've never seen the sunshine
Nor the clear blue sky
But I've never had the feelings
That I'm left out and want to die

I can sense and touch the elements
I can feel and know the colours
I can hear and smell the air
I feel the wind going through my hair

People look and stand me out
I can't see them so I can't shout
But I'm not different
because
We all do have a Mother
So that makes me
The same as all the others.

Claire Thomson, Stirlingshire

IVORY TOWERS

Beneath the dreaming spires we climbed
To turreted rooms with tutors blind,
Defending their opinions, deflecting our attack,
Astride their hobby horses,
Jousting in the dark.

Truth, lies and videotape combine with papers read,
Thinkers who are living, philosophers who are dead,
Questions have no answers, black is black or white
Freedom can be slavery, blindness never sight.

Tutorials are over, closed doors are open wide,
Down twisted spiral stairwells we hurry out of sight,
Hurry into different worlds with others that we share,
Making sense of life and loss and castles in the air.

Janette Martin, Glasgow

Dedicated to the memory of my mother Margaret Parker and for Mary and Una who "climbed the stairs" with me.

Janette Martin said: "I have been scribbling for as long as I can remember and Ivory Towers was written while studying philosophy as a mature student at university. I was eager to learn, but disillusioned to find that most academics were not the superman I had thought them to be. I am married with two grown up daughters and a brilliant threeyear-old granddaughter, Katie. John and I enjoy renovating our sprawling old home, exploring and working our team of sled dogs. I am a keen family historian and enjoy giving tours around a local museum."

MUSING ON A NOVEMBER MORNING

Two white doves flitting out
Oblivious both of heartache
That's lurking just behind.
Gray, opaque and dank the sky
While they, the sufferers,
Bear the yoke below.

Knowing not the sufferers,
Knowing not the doves,
Knowing not the writer,
Still the urge to be.

Sandgrains on the beach
The wind to blow the storm.
The wind to blow from point to point
And point to point and back;
Yet still the sand and still the doves,
Strong, white; until the everlast.

John Norman Webster, Edinburgh

John Norman said: "I am an emigre Yorkshireman who
came to live in Scotland in 1962 when I was 25 years old.
Now retired from my professions of lecturing and teaching,
I live in a suburban house in the south of Edinburgh. My
surroundings were not always suburban, as I have lived
and worked in Kitimat and Dawson Creek in Canada,
Melbourne in Australia and Galloway and the Moray Firth
in Scotland. I have a keen interest in nature and the out-
doors. I am married with four children and have seven
grandchildren."

CORAL BEACHES

Pale ochre shoreline
Composed of crushed shells
Turquoise at high tide.

James Bennett, Falkirk

GRIEF

I will wait for the morning sun
and leave the grieving for the darkest night.
When only the stars will see my tears
as I grieve alone in the pale moonlight.

I will rise and greet another day
and observe the usual conventions.
I will smile and nod to each one I meet
and hide my pain,
to escape from their attentions.

then when I'm alone I will think of you
and the mask will slip.
Tears held back will start to flow
and the ice from my heart will slowly drip,
as grief and anger will surely melt
and my pain and anguish can again be felt.

Nothing matters, nothing makes sense.
I will remain aloof, my only defence.
Perhaps then they'll go and leave me alone;
alone with my pain, to deal with my grief,
that has stolen my life like an invisible thief.

Mary Wylie, Falkirk

AN UNFRIENDLY SKY

Words on a hillside written in stone,
Dedicated to someone who died here alone,
Far from his family, far from his friends
On a sad pilgrimage to a peace without end.

Withering blossoms brought here to lie
Near the spot where his body was found in July.
Family grieving, wondering why
Their son chose to die 'neath an unfriendly sky.

This world is a harsh battleground for the young.
Black clouds of despair often block out the sun.
What dark demons drove you alone here to die
So far from your home 'neath an unfriendly sky?

Rosemary Thomson, Wishaw

THE DYING SWAN

Bright as a flame, light as air
She drifted gracefully here and there
Her arms round and slender, her body light
She was such a beauteous sight.

There had been no one to compare
With her artistry so fair
So you'll never see her like again
She really was beyond our ken

She called for the costume of the dying swan
But was too weak to put it on
The saddest telegram I've always thought
Bore the words , Pavlova mort.

Dorothy Robb, Edinburgh

GREEN EYES

Memory after memory
pass through my skin when I dance for you.
Memory after memory
travels my blood
picking flowers for your smile.
Tell me how I still
the aching frames within my neurons.

Erna Horn, Gorebridge

THE FIRE

Our attention waits
For flame after flame
Primeval darkness surrounds us
All alone on the edge

Red darts thrust to the sky
Drowning out the stars of light
The land folds out
And we are on the edge.

Reality and truth means everything
With the possibilities they bring
For flame after flame
Reveals the truth

That is reality.
That is the fire.

Everything is not as it seems
For the world is full of forgotten dreams.

Andrew V Schurei, Inverness

WHERE THE MILLWHEEL TURNS

This poem is country, country is poetry too.
Breeze style, a stile to leap con brio,
And where the millwheel turns we'll meet.

Ponderous, rushy fen-side plodded ennui-o,
Mysterious, misty glen, lost our bearings,
This poem is country, country is poetry too.

Cheerful, hill summit gained 'mid cheering,
Blue mere, lark rising oh so heavenward,
And where the millwheel turns we'll meet.

Brown moor, curlew calling deep in colour,
The trails leafy matting squelch, mouldy odour.
This poem is country, country is poetry too.

Pine needles' pungent carpet, scent neath feet,
Rest by the brook then race thro the bracken,
And where the millwheel turns we'll meet.

Below in the village the pace will slacken,
Beside mill-race old inn with rustic seat,
This poem is country, country is poetry too,
And where the millwheel turns, both meet.

J H McGibbon, Glasgow

THE DRIFTER

I'm in and out of spaces and places
Wonder If I'm really there or somewhere
Else, for where is here, are you there my dear?
Am I you or am I me or should I just wait and see?

Is what I do real or illusion?
Is this a result of inner confusion?
Is there inside me someone else, maybe I am just the
pulse?
I'm in and out of spaces and places

Innocent minds and empty faces, reality traces
Are others observant of what I say, does it cause dismay?
I'm in and out of spaces and places
Wonder if I'm really there? I must be somewhere.

Jonathan Muirhead, Edinburgh

Jonathan Muirhead was born in Edinburgh. Jonathan
enjoys writing, listening to music, films and debating. "I
started writing poems when I was 13 years old, because I'd
always enjoyed writing stories at school," he remarked. "My
work is influenced by music, moods and the work of Edwin
Morgan and other writers. My style is acerbic, thoughtful
and concise. I would like to be remembered as one who
thought deeper than most and was kind and thoughtful
towards others." Aged 23 he is a civil servant with an ambi-
tion to publish a novel and make a film. He has written
over 300 poems and had many published, including his
own collection, "Inside My Head" available at £3.00 plus
£1.50 p and p from 38711 Gorgie Rd, Edinburgh.

SOUL OF THE HIGHLANDS

I am the breath of ancient times.
I am the soul of the Highlands.
I am consciousness divine.
I am the soul of the Highlands.

The blood in my veins are the rivers clear.
My bones are the mountains, solid and strong
My features were cut from cliffs so sheer.
My voice, the wind, sings my Highland song.

The little lochens, a thousand eyes,
Watch over all life, be it great or small.
My body, the earth, lets you realise,
If you treat it correctly, there is food for all.

My hands, the trees, I lift up high,
Pointing the way to the stars.
And to the Creator I pray and sigh:
Keep my Highlands safe, no more wars.

Helga Dharmpaul, Tain

A MAN'S LAST PRAYER

As he lay filthy, rotting, excrement, mingled with his blood,
Shackled tightly to the prison wall, like an ape kept for
experiment to save the human race
His head twisted by an iron spiked collar like a man with
no identity,
A man with no face,
He looked up whispering, Oh Lord keep me in your grace,
Forgive me for my sins "God did your son Jesus feel the
nails going into him when put on the cross to die?
Did he cry? "Forgive them for what they do" the politicians
that's who. I was one, till the red army came, I took the
blame
Life in this country will never be the same,
Now I'm here a Prisoner of conscience sent to die in this
pox ridden jail - my faith in God will not fail, as my time on
earth, comes to an end, may I find peace in heaven,
And Christ be my friend"

Catherine Kane, Glasgow

Catherine Kane said: "I was born in Glasgow and my hob-
bies are American quilting, art and music. I have written
40 poems and had five published. I have sole copyright of
'A Man's Last Prayer'. At present I am studying psychology
and counselling. My writing is realistic, based on my life's
experience while living in the outback of Ghana, West
Africa. I am proud of my ability to write poetry and I hope
to sell my work in book form and gain recognition, poetry is
a gift to be used and enjoyed."

BRING TAE ME YOUR BAGPIPES

Bring tae me your bagpipes.
And we can play a tune,
We'll play it at daybreak,
We'll play it a noon,
We'll play it in the cold December,
Or in the hottest June,
We'll play for it beneath the stars,
Or the silvery moon,
We'll play for princesses and Czars.
We'll play for the urchins in the street,
Who never get enough to eat
We'll play it for the butcher
Who gives us our daily meat,
We'll play it for the old maids
And watch them tap their feet,
The pibroch and the chanter,
Or e'en the humble drone
For when you play the bagpipes
No man is alone.

Alan Pow, Roxburghshire

SONG OF THE WHALE

Sonar booms in the dark blue sea
I hear the Beluga calling me
Through the tempest storm and gale
I hear the haunting song of the whale

Large grey humpback blowing free
Diving and rising in the surging sea
From Arctic wastes and sunset pale
I hear the haunting song of the whale

Lord and Master of the deep
The portals on Neptune's kingdom keep
Thrashing asunder from head to tail
I hear the haunting song of the whale

Entombed in oceans wide and deep
By man his filthy lucre reap
As hunters seek their Holy Grail
I hear no more the song of the whale.

James Adams, Dundee

I'LL STAND IN LINE

At half past nine I stood in line and watched him leave that
one last time.
Those years we laughed and quaffed and watched our
game, a fair result our only aim.
Perhaps a hint of blue crept in but this was not a mortal
sin.
It shouldn't be that this should end, has every road to have
a bend but what a road and what a life.
Perhaps we all should aim to strive, to leave a memory, so
alive.
I knew that when he gave that wave that he would shortly
take his leave and not to grieve would be his wish.
So play that song just one more time, think back on years
and happier clime.
Fond memories run through my mind.
All in good time but just for now
I'll stand in line.

John Thompson, Clarkston

*The night my neighbour and lifetime friend Bert passed
away, I felt the need to write these lines.*

IN THE COUNTRY

The sweet smell of wild flowers
Blowing in the breeze
The wind sounding like voices
Echoing between the trees
A summer's day sun beating down on your back
Walking in the county you're on the right track.

Two horses playing in the field
The farmer struggling to bring in his yield
Birds flying majestically in the sky
A little mouse hiding in the rye

Fish swimming in the river
Some ducks all in a quiver
Anglers angling on the river edge
Crows crowing in the thicket hedge

Mother Nature's wonders are there for all to see
So go for a walk in the country
And fill your heart with glee
And the best thing about it is it's absolutely free.

Mick McCartney, Milton

Born in Glasgow, **Mick McCartney** enjoys running and coaching athletics. "I started writing poetry a year ago for a pastime and my work is influenced by everyday happenings. I try to tell a story in rhyme and I would like to be remembered as someone who appreciated life." Aged 46 he is an information technology worker with an ambition to win the veteran running championship and to publish a book. He is married to Trisha and they have two children, Michael and Sharon. "The person I would most like to meet is Nelson Mandela and the person I would most like to be for a day is Bill Gates. I have written many poems and had a couple published and I have also written short stories."

FREEDOM

As the mist rolled down, the bracken glen
And the fish leaped in the loch
I gazed upon its eerie shore, at a castle
And its broch

A vision of a highland man appeared
Before my eyes
his tartan plaid, windswept and torn
His claymore reaching to the skies

Who was this man in tartan clad
This vision that I'd seen
Standing proudly by a cairn
Where the croft he lived, had been.

Was this a message from the past
To remind us how to fight
No claymores needed for to win
As independence is now in sight.

Patrick Doolan, Glasgow

LIVING IN THE SHADOW OF SILVER BEAUTY

The silver dragon has spread her wings
She is only small, but growing well
I'd turned my face from her and all other things.
But, I am drawn still into her spell

As a child I knew her well
Cold skin grey eyes and gleaming teeth
She lacked colour or flare. I could not tell
What treasures lay beneath

Through selfish eyes I viewed this beast
Imposing what little personality I had
I look now, older and wiser. I look to share
The pleasures to be had.

Robin Thornton, Banchory

Born in Barrow, **Robin Thornton** enjoys combining his music and literary talents in the form of songwriting. "I started writing poetry at the age of eight," he remarked. "The psychological character traits of a childhood medical disorder had manifested themselves in an ability to write. That disorder is called hydrocephalus. Largely my work is influenced by friends and my style is lyrical, cryptic and enigmatic. I would like to be remembered as a writer who brought hydrocephalus to the public eye." Aged 23 he is a reception temp with an ambition to shake free from the shackles of ordinary work and sell songs for a living. He has written several poems and had one published. He has also written articles on music.

CHRISTMAS MAGIC

Do you believe in Santa Clause,
The reindeer and the elves,
That work so hard throughout the year,
To stack up Santa's shelves.

When you are tucked up in your bed,
Listening for Santa's sleigh,
And dreaming of the present in your stocking on Christmas
day,
Do you believe that Santa down the chimney comes,
With dolls and games and sweets and toys,
And skates and bikes and drums.

Do you believe the Christ child,
Was born on Christmas day,
The Ox, the ass, the cattle, the manger where he lay.

If you believe in all these things,
You'll know the magic that only Christmas brings.

Margaret Blake, Ross-Shire

For George, Kerry, Kelsey, Reegan, Louis. A memory from Gran. For Noel, my brother, for the Christmases we missed sharing.

Born in Yorkshire, **Margaret Blake** enjoys reading, writing, theatre, walking and swimming. "I started writing in school and carried on afterwards," she said. "I find it relaxing and also I write comic verses for friends." My work is influenced by a word, a garden, a scene, or anything that can inspire me to start scribbling." Margaret is a care worker with an ambition to write a funny book. She is married to Ken and they have four children. "The person I would most like to be for a day is Lily Savage because he's got a better figure than me! I have written lots of poems but this is the first time I have had one published. I have also written a pantomime and I am working on a book," she added.

VISIONS OF ALBA

Looking over the hills, I see
The land as it used to be.
Clansmen resting in the glen,
Next to their but-Ben,
Women collecting peat
For fires where they cook their meat,
The stag standing as proud as can be
While the deer look on with curiosity.
Over the hills clansmen march,
Their plaids showing many colours,
Clashing against the purple heather.
The golden eagle soaring up high,
Confident he is king of the sky.
The highland cattle, a sight to behold,
With his long fur against the cold.
My Vision fades and I lift my wee dram
And think with sorrow of a great time gone by.

Billie Healy, Cumbernauld

A NATURE DISCOVERY

My son found a lovely rose,
But stuck the damn thing up his nose,
Alas, he found this was quite sore,
So he doesn't do this anymore.

Charlie Stuart, Peterhead

THE EDUCATION OF THE POET

The poet lives a lonely life, you said,
gives up the day and borrows half the night,
stakes out his soul to earn his daily bread.

You said I need to read before I write.
Good grief, does "all my life" not qualify?
My bursting throat, my head stuffed full of light

and instant language? Forgive my sigh.
Pulp fiction and the fruits of rarer gift
clutter my bed, climb up behind my eye

and glimmer into dawn. They skim and drift,
they lure me on, these jostlings from the dead,
to serve the watch, to carry out my shift
and pitch my boat against the fountainhead.
The poet's is a risky life, you said.

Josephine Brogan, Edinburgh

PARENTS

You cared for me for many years
Through times of joy and times of tears
Always there to help me through
Trying to keep me honest and true

Along the way I failed at times
I paid dearly for my 'crimes'
You always picked me up and said,
"Take the lesson as read"

I matured at last and grew wiser
It is my turn now to be your adviser
To care for you in winter years
To help you with your troubles and fears.

Ann C Todd, Sauchie

PEACE ON EARTH

Let the world have harmony and peace
As it should rightly be,
Let all war and conflict cease
And just have ceremony.

Let s enjoy life to the full
With love and liberty,
Oppression the exception, not the rule
With all the people free.

When we are born, until we're dead
'Tis a short eternity,
Everyone knows that blood is red
Why spill it unnecessarily.

David Holmes, Selkirk

CONSEQUENCE

A tender child, A world apart
The beating of a mournful heart
Orphans of the souls that die
The intake of a breathless sigh.

Holding close but travelling far
The cut will heal but leaves a scar.
Parents leave a world of vex
And the consequence of sex.

Tomorrow is just another day
But not for them who hope and pray.
To burst with life and breath the air
Of parents who both love and care.

Although we are just grains of sand
We have emotions, loving hands.
A new born baby always cries
But what about the one that dies.

James Lunan, Port Glasgow

FIRST LOVE

It was by chance, that we did meet
When I fell accidentally at her feet
It was plain for all to see
As I landed on my knee
When I looked up to my surprise
I could see into her eyes
They were twinkling like the stars
Was I on planet earth or on mars?

Then as I got to my feet
I felt my heart had skipped a beat
Taking time to recover
I felt I could really love her
That body of hers, so slim and slender
She is just so warm and tender
A beautiful woman through and through
I would give all my love to you.

Jack Dobbin, Greenock

A NEED FOR A SISTER

I'm sitting here and wondering
Just what you'd be like
Tall and skinny, same as me
Or little, fat and round
Pleasant spoken every word,
Not that I'm that loud.

Trying hard to make people proud
We'd help each other to please the crowd
I'm really not that bothered
As long as you were here
Giving me your shoulder
and wiping away that tear.

Rose Graham, Kilsyth, Glasgow

SPRINGTIME

The earth is in slumber, and patiently waiting,
and holds dear the secrets of coming rebirth.
Silently, slowly she starts to awaken
from out of the long, cold, dark winter of death.

Through snowfalls and windstorms the strength is discov-
ered:
the will to live on, and rejoice in the living.
Earth will survive all the efforts of Winter,
and offer her beauty to all, in forgiving.

The tree's naked branches adopt a new fashion:
overnight, as it seems, the buds start to form.
While under a blanket of Autumn's old colours.
the stirring of snowdrops tell Springtime will come.

Helen Gavin, Lanarkshire

THE OLD FIR

Sink your teeth in
Deep enough to draw blood.
Drink to refresh your green cloak
That hides an ageing brown skeleton.
Shake your head in the night
Scratching claws across my window.
Spit venom at innocence
Tempted by juicy wheals.
Burn the hands of all
That try and reach your soul.
Yet when the woodcutter
Stakes your blackened heart:
I'll cry, for I've lost
The terror of childhood.

Claire Wightman, Aberdeenshire

WINTER'S DREAM

Crumbled snow like falling dreams
Bursting on the tips of fairytale spires.
The acid moon drips milky white,
Diffusing clouds of midnight marble.

Behind the theatre, citrus lamplight
Spatters in glowing pools of damp.
Ghost carriages rumble up the terrace.
Echo of hooves ringing in the history

Of a winter's dream, forgotten paradise,
Centuries of people span the frozen river,
Forbidding gothic arch pointing to heaven,
Haven in the heart of an icy granite fantasy.

Karen Lisa Ryley, Aberdeenshire

GREGOR'S ARRIVAL

He arrived on Tuesday, 13th May,
A bundle of pink, baby snuffles,
Black hair, big eyes, surprised look around
As he entered a big world full of sound.

His Mum is Ruth, his father, Gordon,
And both are quite ecstatic!
For Gregor Alexander's come
To make a family, he's number one.

But I'm not his mother or father either,
I'm the Gran, some four daughters wiser,
But I've been touched again by love
Of this tiny baby come from above.

Our grandson's birth, so filled with longing,
Has brought such joy, I've never stopped telling
Friends and neighbours of this dear boy
Who's filling life with special joy.

So if you catch me smiling quietly
With a precious tiny in my arms,
You'll know it's being a Gran that makes
This world so wonderful, see my face!

Elizabeth Sudder, Aberdeenshire

KITTENS

My little jewels important to treat the same.
To give you each a characteristic dominant name.
Five adorable kittens born without a flaw.
Now cat-like prowl on silent velvet paw.
Stealthily you perceive with bright eyes.
Majestic immodesty you sway tail held high.
Apt names of gems I chose for you.
Coincided personalities and hue.
Amber your ambitious and agile,
Jade a duchess with elegant style.
Topaz just playful and introvert.
Tiger-I alert quick hunter to kill,
Ebony, sable seeking panther-like will.
My little kittens grown into cats.

Yvonne Fraser, Perth

Yvonne Fraser said: "I was born in Dundee and I am a
registered childminder living in Perth. My hobbies include
writing poetry, Scottish history, and genealogy. I married
my pen pal Ian James McKenzie and through writing let-
ters my love of poetry grew. With Ian's encouragement I
have had over 50 poems published in various anthologies.
Words put together can express my personal thoughts by
penning onto paper. My ambition is to live life to the full
and achieve all that I can."

OOR FANNY

Oor sister Fanny was always sae canny
She vowed she'd no look at a man
Yin day she got foo coming hame frae the brew
And finished up marryin' Tam
Noo Tam was a farmer and he had to learn her
A' the things tae dae on the farm
She'd milk Daisy the coo
While Tam followed the ploo.
And when darkness fell he'd come hame tae feed Nell
His auld sheep dog in the barn.

Betty Wilson, Wigtownshire

SILENT BELL

She is loyal and true
She is beautiful too,
I can always rely,
As each day goes by,
For her to be there,
Emotions stripped bare,
No loneliness for me,
For I know she will be,
Trying to please,
To put me at ease,
She is not selfish or vain,
She keeps me sane,
Friendship so deep,
Good memories to keep,
When my bell doesn't ring,
She can make my heart sing,
Enriched day by day,
My pet shows the way.

Isabel Taylor, Cumbernauld

THE BEACH

The beach is fun when you run
On the soft sandy sand.
The tide comes in and the tide goes out.
all day long one can paddle about.

The waves are splashing and crashing
on the rocks.
Creatures coming out of their shells,
put your ear down on the ground hear the magical ringing
sounds
The soft cool air hits off your face and you think to your-
self.
Oh my, what a lovely place

Lorraine Arkley, Inverkip

WHY

Why are we so easily led
When half the world never gets feed
Why are so greedy
When half the world are needy.

Why are we so cheerful
When half the world is tearful
Why do we have fun
When half the world has none.

Why are we so glad
When half the world is sad
So why don't we give
So half the world can live
So why.

William Dyer, Clacks

MIND GAMES

I don't want to write this, well yes. maybe I do
But do I really want to share these thoughts with you?
Tell you about the things that make me want to scream?
Ask if you can understand my dreams
Dare I let mask fall?
Bare my inner self to all
Or continue as before
And stay behind my tightly closed door.

Margaret Thomas, Midlothian

MEMORIES DUSTED

In the attic, dust has settled
Upon wood and metal.
Things forgotten.
Kept for a rainy day.
Brought down in May.
Annual spring clean.
Attic is kept, for things that are kept.
For children of children
Not yet born,
Hat boxes brim loaded
Lids not closing, homes for spiders
Never disturbed till memories dusted.
Creaks the attic door.
Remember this remember that,
Coppertone picture of wide brimmed hats.
Dress with bustle.
Must be nice.
Hear the rustle,
When memories stirred
In the attic.

William Morran, Renfrew

SPECIAL FRIENDS

Although my love for you is a statement
This just happens to be true
The best husband and friend, I ever had
I'm happy to say is you
You were always there, when I needed you
Then you turned, and went away
I knew, I could not depend on you
At any time of day
1998, had its ups and downs
As just about everyone does
But problems, rarely last this long
With special friends, like us
I love you deeply, within my heart
And this will always stay
I will not share you, with anyone else
So please, just stay away.

Josephine MacDonald, Perth

SPRINGTIME

Listen to the earth awaking
Listen to the voice of spring
Listen to the blackbird singing
Listen as the lark takes wing

Smell the sweetness of the violet
Smell the perfume of the whin
Smell the earth awakening
Shaking off her winters sleep

Feel the softness of the calkins
trembling in the morning breeze
feel the miracle of springtime
fulled with wonder such as these.

Jean Nutt, Ross-shire

THE SEA

What appeals always to me, is the magnificent,
mighty sea.
It is so powerful to behold whilst retaining
mysteries yet untold.
Standing observing its vast domain, inwardly
revives me again and again.
I never weary of that splendid sight, which induces sheer
delight.
Thus I promise never to stray, far from its sublime vicinity,
Just to be there in its presence is of total bliss the essence.
In all its moods, its resounding refrain proclaims its auton-
omy will ever remain
Truly every sighting is one of profound admiration for that
eternal saline manifestation.

Helen Allan, Glasgow

56

FIRST DAY AT SCHOOL

My alarm goes off one hour early
I'm so excited my hair goes curly
My heart is thumping really fast
And by this time its quarter past

I'm in the bus and I feel really small
They must be third years they look so tall
I sit put in a seat quiet and shy
And at this moment I feel I could die

Half the day has gone past
I feel I have learned more at last
It's time to go home and I feel so cool
And now I say, school does rule

I go to my bed and have a good nights sleep
The alarm then goes off BEEP BEEP BEEP
I then realise that it was all a dream
And I want to go back now because I'm keen.

Claire Thomson, Aberdeenshire

HAPPINESS AND SADNESS

Dewdrops caught
in the spiders web
a string of diamonds

Dewdrops caught
in the spiders web
a string of tears.

Stephen Rae, Ayr

THE MONEY

I'm simply am invention that has become a need,
A subject of contention in every case of greed,
A symbol of the value, a value of the things,
Disputed at the venues by paupers, traders, kings

I generate just quarrel and tension, even war,
When used beyond the morals, the reason or the law.
Because of me there's murder and wickedness and lie,
Unwillingly I further the honesty to die.

I can adjust a union, a marriage, or a pact,
I set up the communion of interests in effect;
From man to man I'm passing, if they are good or worse
I don't mind, for my crossing is meant to stuff their purse.

Some say that I am evil while others say I'm good,
Some think I'm rather trivial, depending on their mood.
Whatever name I'm given I'm sure of one thing:
Through people I have thriven as their real king.

Eugenia Popescu, Aberdeenshire

CATTOLICA CAPER

Drinking wine at "Tre Piccioni"
Of troubles, cares we hadna' ony
Until it came to foot the bill
The prospect made us feel quite ill
For it was double what we thought
What could be done? We'd quaffed the lot
And so, to h_ _l about tomorrow
We bought some more to drown our sorrow.

Margaret McClelland, Ayr

BETWEEN THE TICKS OF THE CLOCK

Floating dreams amidst discarded thoughts.
Translucent promises,
From one that should know.
Wafting fragrance from hidden flower.
Moments without words,
Between the ticks of the clock.

Capricious lights, suspending dreams
In this mysterious space.
Light years to the stars,
Gravity destroys time.
Is this now or before?
Between the ticks of the clock.

After is too late
Before is to soon.
Now is when it should be.
Time is not here or there,
It is just in the mind.
The clock ticks on.

Christine Pond, Kirkbean

ELECTRIC STORM

Your love strikes like, thunder and lightning
Leaves me stunned, still standing
Roaring out a warning then burning me with a start
Ricocheting and piercing directly in my heart
Shocked by the ferocity of its tenderness
Bewildered at first, I accept togetherness
A static intertwining of lightning strike forms
I dream of always feeling these electric storms.

John Fraser Hynd, Fife

FORCE EIGHT

The storm blew up in the early afternoon
Waves white-crested, boist'ring up the Firth,
Gaining momentum, height and strength
The day chilled in the darkening gloom.

Reefed down, a yacht speeds up the Clyde,
Disappearing at times through cloud and spray,
A naval destroyer grey on grey seas
Punches its way through wind and tide.

A young man, sea-slicked, laughter burbling
In his throat, runs with a black dog
Yapping and jumping at his sleeve,
Side-leaping the waves that claw greedily
At his feet.

Shingle splatters on to the prom,
Spume flies, like detergent through the air,
Stinging rain nettles our faces,
Thrilled by the tempest we sing our way home.

Sheila MacFarlane, Largs

THE SQUIRREL

Whisky, frisky, hippity hop,
Up he goes to the tree top.
Whirly, Twirly round and round,
Down he scampers to the ground.
Furly curly, what a tail.
Tall as a feather, broad as a sail.
Where's his supper? In the shell,
Snappity crackity. Out it fell.

Lucy McManus, Edinburgh

UNREMARKABLE WITHOUT

I'm not the first star to be seen
I am the last to say what I mean
I'm not the first to break the rules
I am the last to get to choose
I'm not the first snowflake to melt
I am the last one who gets help
I'm not the first tear to be shed
I am the last one to be heard
I'm not the first broken heart to be mended
I am the last one to be defended
I'm not the first to accomplish a dream
I am the last to be chosen for the team
I'm not the first to be remembered at all
I am the last to make it over the wall
I'm not the first choice on the list
I am the last one who is missed
I'm not the first to be in demand
I am the last to make a stand
I'm not remarkable
Without you.

Elaine Donaldson, Peterhead

WHAT IS A POEM?

A poem is something filled with joy
It's the smile on the face of every girl and boy
A poem will brighten up your day
It is a story told in a special way
Some poems mean love,
Some poems mean hate,
Some mean luck
And some mean fate
But every word says something new
It's a gift put in rhyme especially for you.

Samantha Osborne, Cumbernauld

Samantha Osborne said: "I have been writing verse for two years now and 'What is a Poem?' expresses how I feel about poetry. It is a privilege to have one of my poems published as I am only 12 years old and started secondary school this year. I live with my mum, dad and older brother and I enjoy reading playing badminton and meeting up with my friends. I have written many other poems and hopefully I will become successful with them as well."

A BOY

A baby son I have you see
And proud of him as I can be
He's tall and handsome
Neat and smart
For he's the one who shares my heart

From baby to a toddler
Then on to pre-school days,
School at primary level
Follows on so fast, remember.
The tie was always crooked
And the shirt it was untucked
With muddy knees on trousers
Which covered up the RIP
"It wasn't me what done it
It was a big football
That bounced right up and hit me,
So hard it made me fall".

They grew up so fast, so hold on tight
For childhood days fade out of sought
They're grown and now the circles tip
And time is round to start again
Our children's children begin again.

Carol Seivewright, West Lothian

POWER

Governments come and go,
But still the facts remain the same.
Their main preoccupation's
To win power once again.

Power through the Generals.
Power through the poll.
It all comes down to weapon piles
Or millions on the dole.

Power through the police.
Power through the courts.
It all comes down to civil strife
And injury reports.

Power through the censor.
Power through the pen.
That all comes down to lies,
They're misleading us again.

I used to think democracy,
Meant power even spread.
Long live democracy.
My democracy is dead.

John Macdonald, Annan

FLIGHT OF FANCY

How many times from the corner of an eye
Is glimpsed a shape, to turn and find it gone.
Or listening, hear above the crashing waves
A seal's cry, or is it a mermaid's song?

A sense of being watched, but no-one's there,
A scent, a flash of colour out of true.
That childhood friend, your partner in crime,
Although unseen by anyone but you.

How to explain a place in every detail known
Though never visited by you before.
A deserted house, beauty surrounds its shell,
But no birds sing, there is sorrow within its core

Perhaps a wish to wonder, instead of know.
To feel things strange instead of see them clear.
Or is it a sight across the stream of time
Of truths existing in another sphere.

Eleanor Hamilton, Tain

A SILENT PARTNER

The music usually ends between two and four.

When I am awake I talk to myself
hearing the sound of my words bounce
from the stained wine glass to the roughly laid sheet.

Hollow bars that carry a message in a bottle.

Sometimes it is when I reach from sleep
to touch her, to smell her skin
cupping the warmed groove around my face
falling into the tread cast behind her retreat.

Beyond the flickering bulb that hangs above the hall
no carpeted steps raised on cistern swell
silence where there ought to be something.

A mumbled phrase, a laboured movement, something.

The sounds that can only exist
when your world stills to frozen, you hear them all.

> *The crack of cotton as hand reaches clock*
> *bellow of pillow as head is raised to chore*
> *distant rumble as tank empties into drain*
> *the click of coffee brought to boil.*

The songs we sing in our mind, when the music forgets to play.

Alexander Cuthbert, Glasgow

Born in Anstruther, **Alexander Cuthbert** enjoys hill walking and bar-room-metaphysics. "I started writing poetry in my early teenage years to find a way to articulate the words which I could not tell but refused to be silenced by self-doubt. My work is influenced by Beckett, Blake and Camus and my style is developing at, as Sartre states, a form of secondary action, action by disclosure." Aged 27 he is a social care worker with an ambition to write at a proficiency which would allow more experimental forms to evolve from his work. "My biggest nightmare is that my disability, Glaucoma, worsens before something truly memorable flows from my pen," he added.

WILL OF A CHILD

When I'm grown up and I die
They will burn me and you will cry,
But don't be too sad when I'm gone
For I know I'll live on,
As long as you remember and care
I know and you know I'll always be there.
So lock me safely in your heart,
And let no one tear us apart.
I know I'll always stand by you,
So prove to me that our friendship's true.

Anna Mathers, Aberdeen

PYLONS FROM OUTER SPACE

They stride along the hill
Monsters from outer space.
Huge and ugly they stand,
Members of an alien race.

These six armed giants
Gunslingers facing a duel.
Waiting to draw their guns,
Against enemies so cruel.

As we travel down the road,
They follow us in our way.
Never out of our sight,
From hill to hill they sway.

Strung together, one to one.
A hideous string of beads.
Looming large against the sky
These outlandish crossbreeds.

Margaret C Rae, Lanarkshire

DEAR GRAN

Its hard to imagine I've left it too late
We seem to believe that these things can wait.
Cruel life, it has shown that this is not true
So I should have known my time left with you
Was fleeting and brief, as life always is.
Who knew of the grief, or the moments we'd miss.
To say that I'm sad and sorry is true
The nice times we had were rare, and I too
Wish you were here still to share more with me.
But please wait until I've said all to thee.
Those three little words so easy to say.
Neither'd be first to ease either's way.
And now you're not here. Too late? maybe true
But, please say you hear, Dear Gran, I love you.

Jane Thomson, Alloa

SUMMER GARDEN

Poppies red, and iris blue
What a medley of colour comes to view
Purple chives and daisies tall
Snap dragons against a wall.

A garden in summer a joy to behold
A tranquil scene, more precious than gold.
Scented roses, the hum of bees
Birds singing among the trees.

Hydrangea coming into bloom
Nature's harmony in tune.
All this surrounds our living space
An oasis from life's hectic pace.

Sheila Macmillan, Inverness

THE TREE OF CHRISTMAS

Behold the beauty of my form,
Spruce green and tapered tall,
Sweet nature's gift to seasons joy,
A grace to cot and hall.

Crimson crossed with berried spray,
From wind whipped countryside,
Tinsel strewn in scattered streams,
As path of heav'ns collide.

Around my feet are laid the gifts
For commoner or king,.
As like the magi to the babe,
From whom our faith doth spring

As I stand amidst you all,
Fresh comes from Gods good earth,
Reminder of a truth clear lit,
Reminder of that birth.

Ra Sefako, Isle of Cumbrae

HEAR WITH THE EAR OF YOUR HEART

Hear with the ear of your heart
And you will know you are a part,
Of all that is goodness and light.
A star shining and ever bright.
At one with all spiritual essence,
An essential, magnificent presence.

Catherine Seiler, Aberdeenshire

DAWN

In the dawn's early light
On a hill top high
They crucified our Lord
And watched him die

The pain that he bore was
For all humanity, his sweat
Turning to drops of blood
Cleansing both you and me

To him be praise and glory
For he has set us free
Lifting us from bondage
That we may see the light.

M Hardman, Ramsey, Isle of Man

LOVER

Re-awaken me
Rescue me from the dead
Fill me with her vision
In this heart and head
Let me reach out
And touch her skin
Let me feel a naked flame
Burning strong within
Let it wash over me
Like ocean to the shore
Let it surround me
Penetrating to the core
Feel the hunger
After such a great fast
Feel desire upon my lips
Re-awaken at last.

Karen O'Neill, Edinburgh

THE MEEK SHALL INHERIT

The water strokes her mermaid scales
curved like pale water lily petals
as she watches motionless from a rock pool
carved in antediluvian memory.

Seeing through the distortion
of refracted light on cracked glass ripples,
it seems almost beautiful, this world
of upright, walking creatures.

Underwater, her hair teases the seaweed,
a she-tree, swaying in the ebb-tide,
where seahorses shelter
and hermit crabs absail on home-sewn shells.

She sees the chemicals and the oil-slicks
and the cysts on the fishes
and knows that, one day,

When they have plundered their world
Beyond repair or remorse,
she will claim her inheritance.

Alison Tavendale, Aberdeenshire

HARVESTMAN

A special species of spider
Is the harvestman. You may have spotted him,
Splendidly spruce though sprawled on a spade,
His spindly legs spread out like spokes
On a bicycle wheel.

In spite of his being but a speckle
Which a sparrow could scarcely spot,
Spontaneously, he springs to life
And in his specific spidery way
He sprints for home at speed.

Jennifer Brown, Dundee

PADDY THE HORSE

I had a horse when I was young
Paddy was his name, with a big red tongue.

His mane was grey his tail was too
His eyes were bright and shiny blue

We had such fun my horse and I
Big and brown he stood so high

Riding on him every day
I fed him no water not even hay

He wasn't upset, he did not mind
Paddy was a horse of the rocking kind

Although he was wooden, and not a real horse
I was young, and I loved him "of course".

Mary Gemmell, Balloch

THE GLEN OF WEEPING

Sleep well MacDonald in your island grave,
Grieve not for the children you could not save
Birds swoop and cry in remembered pain;
The sisters weep again and again.

In winter's blizzard sharp and snell,
As before the upraised sword you fell,
The guest the enemy became;
To Campbell's everlasting shame.

Helen Dick, Fife

To my Mother Helen Campbell. We both loved Scottish history. Helen lived for 103 wonderful years.

THE ROBIN

The robin comes when autumn's waning,
His red breast fresh with courtship staining,
He marks his boundary and keeps it clear,
Not even the crow, dare go near.

His food secure he takes a mate,
It's not his plan to vegetate,
And when winter is at its height,
He forages daily, with all his might.

This survival plan is on his mind,
And so it is with all his kind,
When winter's o'er and spring is nearing,
The brood in flight and thoughts are cheering,
He'll not return in his bold dress,
Until he wishes to impress.

Montgomery Lindsay, Doune

MY DEAR FRIEND

This time its life is over
Its been with me for years,
The man just took one look,
and told me, my worst fears.

Its had a long life really
My truest dearest friend,
I don't know, what I'll do now
There's nothing that will mend.

I remember when I got it
so clean, and sparkling white,
But I've known, for a few months now,
It was giving up fight.

Well now it's really finished,
This thing that meant so much
My washing machine, has gone and died
and left me in the lurch.

Helen Osborne, Perth

THE DYING FLOWER

It is time for me to depart
whispers the fading flower as her fragile petals fall
lying limply on the ground
Her former beauty
a shroud around her

Her departure is urgent
the ground is calling her
the ground where her seed was germinated is calling
is calling her home.

Jacqui Hogan, Ayrshire

SHADOWS

The shadows we see on the wall
As we sit alone in our rooms.
The flicker we see on the building
As we walk past, in the dark.
These are not a reflection of us,
But memories that follow us around.
Of the things we have done and the
People we have known.

They don't disappear when we forget them.
They follow us around in the darkness,
Looking to be remembered.
But we only see them when we look up too quickly.
Or when they are caught in the candlelight.
You see, we will always just forget them,
But they will always be there.

Sandra MacLean, Ayrshire

LIFE

A new life
A new dawn
Someone finds happiness
Where another is torn
Life is just one big circle
Where one finds happiness
Another will find sadness
Obstacles lie in our path
Overcome them don't turn back.

Victoria Young, West Lothian

AN APOLOGY FROM GOD

Mankind take notice
I wish to apologise
I made a mistake

I must assure you
This failure is not your fault
For I am to blame

My project did fail
And now you're out of control
I must end this now

You will cease to be
In around seven minutes
Again, I'm sorry

Thanks for choosing life
Feel free to visit again
And have a safe trip.

Laura McLeod, Angus

HEAVEN

I wonder what it's like in heaven,
To look down on the stars
And see the clouds go drifting by,
And catch a glimpse of Mars.

Do flowers grow, and grass, and trees,
And lilacs in the Spring,
Some waterfalls, a village green,
And butterflies on the wing?

Happy children, strawberries and cream,
Rabbits, bees and birds that sing
Elephants, deer, a rainbow's beam,
And Sundays when the church bells ring?

Or is there Heaven right here on earth,
With loved ones all around,
The warm sun, the silver moon,
And God's good gifts abound?

Maisie Miller, Broxburn

THE SCOTTISH PLAY

Macbeth, the time is long since past
for your fair name to be cleared at last,
or did you on Will Shakespeare's play
a dreadful curse in vengeance lay
that actors are afraid to say
the title, but rather choose to name
your masterpiece of ancient fame
(for who are they, to take the blame)
The Scottish Play.

Jean Lunan, Perth

THE STRANGER TO THE SUN

The stranger to the sun
Is clothed in darkness
The stranger to the sun
Adversary of the light.

The stranger to the sun
Walks through herds,
The stranger to the sun
This fallen angel.

The stranger to the sun
Contempt for the lights congregation,
Stranger to the sun
Himself his only God.

The stranger to the sun
The fire in the sky his enemy,
The stranger to the sun
Forever will he walk alone.

Chris Clancy, Glasgow

A COLOURED ARCH

Playing in a field one day,
We saw a rainbow far away.
A coloured arch up in the sky,
How it came we wonder why?
No matter how far we ran,
We couldn't find where it began.
Perhaps God sent it from the sky,
We loved it so my friends and I.
Suddenly it must have flown,
We felt so sad so all alone.
Who ever held that rainbow high,
We wished that he had waved goodbye.

Kay Clements, Inverclyde

UNTITLED

If you've never crossed the sea of love
And reached the other side
Don't tell me that I've done wrong
Or that you are so wise.
I don't want to know your reasons
If you've never ridden the storm
And I don't want to hear your answers
If all you've seen is dawn.

If all you've seen is sunshine
How can you hear the rain?
If all your life's been summer
Don't pretend to feel the pain.

Robin Drew, Dundee

ON THIS THEIR WEDDING DAY

The groom stood at the altar
His best man by his side
While down the aisle
With their own special smile
Came two lovely sisters one a bride.

The congregation held their breath
Amidst a scene so dreamy
Had they ever before
Beheld such a vision
As Karen and Kenny's bonnie Jeannie

Then Kenny placed a band of gold
Upon his Jeannie's slender finger
and through all troubles great and small
They both had vowed they'd linger.

and our Lord above
had witnessed all
as heads were bowed to pray
But the proudest were, the parents there
on this their wedding day.

Andrew Lamb, Fife

A MAGICAL LIFE

Magic is the spice of life
Or is the spice of life magic?
If only I knew the answer
Life wouldn't seem quite so tragic.

Some people don't believe in magic
I know I surely do.
If you are still sceptical
Reach out, the Magic will find you.

Amritash Agrawalla, Glasgow

Born in Calcutta, **Amritash Agrawalla** enjoys cricket, cooking, reading and web design. "I started writing poetry in university as a way of expressing myself," he explained. "Through my poems I can say something which is important to me but the reader may see something relevant to them also. My work is influenced by life's experiences and the people I meet. My style is reflective of life and nature. I would like to be remembered as a good and helpful soul always, willing to help." Aged 30 he is a company director with an ambition to be successful and the best at whatever he does. He has written many poems and had several published.

WARZONE

Perpetually falling through cracks in your head
A winding haze through which you are lead
A turning point that doesn't quite turn
But is caged in conflict, sucked in with indifference.

In life there is something about those cracks,
Whose standards are set by our own pride.
An inevitable fate which will drive us mad
Self-creation of lust, condensation of despair.

We feel like we are and we are like we feel
Uniqueness of thought, engulfing the peripheral self,
Solutions are not offered but struggled for and embedded
in
Chinks of light often shattered by darkness.

A preference is not always given, freedom of choice has its
limits
A phobia from which there is no escape: The drowning will
come
To take all that is left
And leave us with nothing but guarded aegis.

Choice, change, co-operation and control
Defining alibis of stability
But what of stability if we are not who we say we are
And if we are, do we stay?

Denise Gildea, Paisley

THE PICKLED MAN

Oh pickled man
Your smile is now as frosty as your face.
You are deceased from the human race.
You stare with eyes of charcoal black.
The fire is still burning in the hearth
Flames dance but you will dance no more.
You are still, your body chilled.
You stare, they stare.
Your glassy eyes are cold, no welcome there.
They look, they learn
They scribble in their grubby pads,
Notes which you cannot read.
You are the thing on which they feed.
Their hungry eyes search the room
In the afternoon gloom.
There in your pickling bag you are.
Is it Malt Vinegar?
Oh! That dissecting knife,
The essence of life.

Wilma Barty, Dumfries and Galloway

APPARITION

She rests against the blossom tree.
Her face composed, not looking at me.
She with her shimmering auburn hair,
A waterfall, cascading, layer upon layer.
And to oppose that, her creamy white skin,
Her elegant figure, so tall and so slim.
The structure of her perfect face,
Holds wisdom and such delicate grace.
Leaning against the apple tree,
My angel, she is so heavenly.

Naomi Howarth, Edinburgh

TO LOVE SOMEONE

To belong to someone, to love someone
Gives all the life you need,
To hate someone, to despise someone
Makes a bitter person indeed.

Ask someone, a lonely one
How much love they need,
You'll find a lonely one
Very heartbroken indeed.

So someone, listen someone
To what I have to say,
Try someone to love everyone
And drive your hate away.

Your love someone given to someone
Will banish your need to hate,
So everyone, "love someone"
Before it grows too late.

D S Anderson, Dumfriesshire

TO CARMEN'S BABY

She lies in her cot,
Unknowing,
Grandparents in grief
Tears flowing.
The sadness of each broken heart,
A mothers bond been ripped apart,
Growing up with thoughts from other,
And their memories of her mother.

Alyson Hunter, Lochgelly

FOR NATALIE

When we were fourteen
Things were so much easier.
All we need worry about was
Make-up, hair and clothes?
Were our faces white enough?
Must keep the brown roots covered,
Maybe a bit more black lipstick?
Had we enough black clothes?
Surely not.

We counted the days till
That Halloween weekend.
We spent the day preparing,
counting the hours
till the night came
when, finally we could make
our debut on
The Goth Scene.

Sara Jane Duffus, Aberdeenshire

A VERSE FOR ANNE

This little verse is written
For you on this special day
As through your life you begin
To gently make your way.

On the road of life
With its many twists and turns
Through all the things you know
And those you have yet to learn.

Through all the laughter
As well as the tears
May God be always with you
To help allay your fears

His eternal glowing light
Always protecting you so
From any harm you encounter
Wherever you should go.

So on this special day
Remember God is there for you
To guide you through life
And make all your dreams come true.

Ian Fowler, West Lothian

DEAR FRIEND

I am writing this poem for you
The one I take my troubles to
Our friendship started when we were little
And we had a few good years
But people move and I suspect
We shed a lot of tears
Then fate stepped in, and in our teens,
We met up once again
And throughout our teenage years
Our friendship did remain
We sailed away on the friendship sea
Then were shipwrecked on the rocky shore of wondering
Were we friends anymore?
The years they came and went
And we'd gone our separate ways
But I always remembered you with the warmth
We'd shared in our halcyon days
Then that mysterious thing called fate, stepped in again
once more
And gave us another chance to get off that rocky shore
So we took the chance and sailed away on that friendship
sea
And can only marvel at the events that have shaped our
destiny.

Lorna Sim, Aberdeenshire

UNTITLED

There it lies
Yellow, black and rotten,
There it lies,
Half eaten, then forgotten.
Left alone to rot in hell,
What will happen?
No one can tell,
There it lies,
Dead as can be,
There it will stay,
For no one can see.

Louise Latto, Fife

Born in Reading in England, **Louise Latto** enjoys walking, poetry, movies, television and football. "I started out in poetry last year and my work is influenced by Dylan Thomas and Emily Dickinson." Aged 21, Louise is a dental assistant with an ambition to be famous. She is single and would like to meet the actor, Mel Gibson. "The person I would like to be most is the poet, Dylan Thomas, so I could see life through his eyes," she said. "I've written over 50 poems but this is the first time I've had one published. I've also written short stories and my autobiography. My biggest fantasy is to be accepted as an actress and poet."

THE GUARDIAN ANGEL

A seagull glided ower th' hoose
Followed shortly by a craw
Baith scroungin' mait fae onyway
Bit oor gairden best o' a'

For I feed th' little birdies
Bits o' fruit an' bits o' bread
Bit they a' tak' t' flight
Fin th' pair are overhead.

They scare aff th' little birdies
Then think, man this is fine
We'll circle roon an' land there
A bountiful place t' dine.

Bit oor yorkie dog thocht different
As they were jist aboot t' land
She shot across th' gairden
Noo th' glove's on th' ither hand.

She trotted awa richt
 prood o' hersel
Th' wee birds thocht her great
A little help fae their guardian angel
Meant they could clear th' plate.

Robbie Innes, Moray

ANGEL

You'll never leave me, this I know,
And safe in this knowledge I shall grow,
Regain my strength, begin again,
Laugh once more, see sun not rain.

You're beauty personified,
Pure energy electrified,
Strength and tenderness all in one,
My moon, my stars, my light giving sun.

You'll always listen when I talk,
Happily come with me on long country walks,
Stand by me in my times of need,
Your presence intoxicates like good Kentish mead.

Around your head, a bright shining aura,
The only clue to your divine power.
Until we were parted I had no cause to believe,
But now you've returned and I've found relief.

You were my moon, my stars, my light giving sun,
Now you're much more - my protector, my angel, my heaven sent one.

Brenda Jane Williams, Clackmananshire

A POEM FOR PETER

We went to the same schools.
I liked him. We played together.
He was a kind giggly shy black boy.
I was a kind giggly shy white girl.

He always came to my birthday parties
That was when he told my mum,
"I'm going to marry your Sue."
He said, giggling, as he ran away...

...feeling shy and embarrassed...
...but he had to say it.

I found out today that he died
Is it true?
He should have stayed in my life
I could have looked after him...

...we would have been all right.

I treasure the memory of
My dear friend Peter Knight.

Sue Ellis, Bonhill

SHETLAND SEA

Sun shining making the sea glisten
Heaven above thinks it must listen
Evening time is a starlight blue
At morning dawn the sun burns through
To shake up the current waves
Looking like horses galloping through caves
And the shore has an angry face
Now the sea calms this place
Displaying all with wonderful grace
That's the Shetland Sea.

Faye Richardson, Shetland

Born in Cambridge, **Faye Richardson** enjoys swimming and athletics. "I started in primary school for a school project and my work was very much influenced by my teacher," she explained. "My style is adventurous and thoughtful and I would like to be remembered as someone who could always make people smile." Aged 11 she is a schoolgirl with an ambition to be an athlete. "The person I would most like to meet is the Queen Mother because she knows so much history. "The person I would most like to be for a day is physical education teacher." Faye has written short stories and a diary as well as many poems. "My biggest fantasy is winning a gold medal in the Olympics," she added.

STARS DANCING

Alone now
I watch the sunburst on azure waters.
The sparkling, incandescent vitality of the sun's rays
exploding on the shimmering surface in a myriad of light,
a vibrant reminder of life.
"Stars dancing...", you said.

A million, twinkling, miniature prisms,
swaying together in magical harmony,
lulled only by the passing breeze.
I am captivated by their beauty,
my senses soothed by their mystical hues.
Entranced by the very wonder of this phenomenon,
my soul moves to its inspiration.

I feel the surge of all encompassing love,
and tranquillity befriends me.
Gentle waves lap the shore of solitude which I now travel,
your stars forever shining to illuminate my path.

When my time comes, I will await you.
Again we shall sit in quiet repose,
encircled in our immortality....
sending our stars to dance for those we love.

Rachel Bodell, Ross-shire

*In memory of Catherine Paterson (1926 - 2001). For all that
you were and are to me. Thank you.*

REMEMBER

Because the time we have is borrowed,
With death one step away,
We should make each second precious,
And be happy while we may.

No tears to blur the memories,
Of tenderness we share,
Just fun and carefree laughter,
And a kiss which says you care.

So wrap your arms around me,
And make me want to stay,
I can't promise you tomorrow,
So remember yesterday.

Glenys Penman, Chryston

To a courageous lady, my friend Michelle Robertson - 9th September 1964 - 12th January 1996. Always remembered.

A JUDGE'S HONOURED THOUGHTS

He is lying, slyly, eyeing, never honestly denying
She is careful, never snareful, often dareful, not unfair
He is clever, miss not a sliver, will he ever, truth deliver
Now she is arty, no, more tarty, a little clarty, cocky smarty

This girl is neat, somewhat petite, with small feet and quite
replete
Would butter melt? or remorse felt, cards rightly dealt,
above the belt
Or cunning, running lie for fun, the battle's won when he is
done
I, inside alone confide, must decide, to run and hide or
reside.

'Twixt wigs and cigs, hopeful digs, scams and rigs, and
mindment figs
She's so stiff, has had a bit, as if he fell off from that cliff
He was drinking, his breath was stinking, it's not linking, I
am thinking
They were loath to take the oath, don't be sloth, jail them
both.

To and fro, and fro and to, to strive to know just what to do
Let's strike a nail on judgments cross, a coin to toss, for
gain or loss
Tepid water, this funny jotter, he has got her like lamb to
slaughter
God and evidence across, the court engross
After all
I am the boss.

William Hamilton, Prestwick

MASK OF AGE

Looking at the mirror
I see sunken, red lined, tired old eyes
Of rheumy washed out blue
Although they are mine
Nothing of me is shining through

They have an empty glaze
As if they look
But do not see
Its hard to accept
That they belong to me.

This craggy old face
Isn't the face I grew up with
It's not a face
My friends would recognise
In it, those empty eyes look at home
All part of the same disguise.

Alexander Mackay, Barrhead

LAUGHTER

I am laughter
I was born a scowl - I really did howl.
And then, I can't remember why I became a smile started
to grow and I developed
into a chuckle
And then, another and another until I was full-blown
laughter.
Winds of mirth howled from me.
I laughed like a drain.
I was laughing gas.
I was an hyena, a jack ass, but never a stock
I surveyed the Earth and saw so many frowns
So many poor sad sorrowful unhappy unfortunate and dull
people
I had to penetrate them, to make them happy and bright
I do this every day
I shall never stop

Mairead Macbeath, Edinburgh

DOES IT MATTER?

Does it matter if people judge you for the colour of your
skin,
Or for your education or for the home you live in?
For different cultures and for different creeds,
Or for how much you have or for how much you need.
Or for your special needs or for your deformities,
Or for your talents or your abnormalities?

Take us as we are and judge us all the same,
At the end of the day we are all human and function with
our brains.
Take us as we are and be happy with what you see,
Do not judge us on what you would like us to be.
At the end of the day does it really matter?

April Uprichard, Lurgan, Craigavon

Born in Belfast **April Uprichard** enjoys swimming, reading
and poetry. "I started writing poetry in 1996 when I had an
encounter with a tramp," she pointed out. "He touched my
heart and I found that poetry was a wonderful way to
express my feelings. I would describe my style as meaning-
ful and deep. If my poetry reaches out to people and touch-
es their hearts that is a wonderful way to be remembered."
Aged 35 she is a care assistant with an ambition to have
her poetry book published. She is married to George and
she has two sons, Andrew and Daniel. "The person I would
most like to meet is the singer Lionel Richie. He has a
unique style and his songs are very touching and meaning-
ful," she said.

SEASHORE PEACE

I like peace
And peace is by the sea
Clear cool water, rocks around;
An overhanging tree.

I like peace
And peace is by the sea

The hills beyond are beautiful
The air is fresh and free
I hear the sound of rushing waves
Talking just for me

I like peace
And peace is by the sea.

Ann Hogarth, Edinburgh

Ann Hogarth said: "I was born in Dunfermline on 21/6/48 to parents Annie and James Muir and grew up in Lochgelly with my two sisters Margaret, Moira and brother Jim. I started writing poetry at the age of 21 years, inspired by pictures and scenery. I have also been inspired and encouraged by friends and colleagues. I married Hamish Hogarth in 1982 and with him I enjoy walking, cycling, travelling around Scotland, caring for my pet dog and cat and fun dog shows. I also enjoy swimming and doing things for charity. I love animals and detest cruelty."

GOD

Through my darkness I have a new sight
that's you my Lord, my beam of light,
You have started up my brand new dreams,
helping me to face my fears,
and pushing away my wasted years.

I'm going to dream without limit and plan
without fear only because you will always be here.
So I bury my sorrows in doing good deeds
like showing my love for others, for that's all anyone needs.

I'll never give up and think I'm through, for there's always
tomorrow and especially there's you,
The love I have for you, it seems, lets me dream my greatest dreams.
The chance at life to grasp again you know you help to ease
all my pain.

Peace be with you

Leigh Stewart, Ballymena

Grandma, we miss you, we love you, we thank you. May God be with you. RIP 5.7.01. Begotten not made.

Born in Belfast **Leigh Stewart** enjoys kickboxing and cycling. "I have found it easy to express myself through poetry throughout my life," remarked Leigh. "My work is influenced by my mother and grandmother and my style is impulsive. I would like to be remembered as a caring, loving and understanding person." Aged 21 he has an ambition to have his own family and be united with his daughter, Jessica. "The person I would most like to meet is Cat Stevens because he is my favourite singer and the person I would most like to be for a day is God. I have written 'Drugs for a Secret Pain' and several poems. This is the second time I have had one published," he added.

A POEM FOR THE DAY

Please remember
That we
Are an army,
Earth itself.
And nothing
Can touch us
That we do not like.
We are a force,
A powerful force
So, please remember:
We're an army
A powerful army.

Jonathan Finlay, County Down

Born in Belfast **Jonathan Finlay** started writing poetry
when he was six. "I did it to entertain my family and
friends," he explained. "I enjoy reading and it gives me
inspiration for my poetry. I think my style is quite imagina-
tive and I would like to be remembered as a poet who
always wrote what he thought." Now aged eight Jonathan
has an ambition to work on children's TV and he would
most like to meet Matthew Corbett, the son of Sooty's cre-
ator. "I would like to be Richard Caddel for a day - because
he is the presenter of the Sooty programme. I have written
several short stories and poems but this is the first time I
have had anything published," he added.

CHRISTMAS MORNING IN DERRY

The dead heads of the hydrangeas, blue-brown
Hang low over the frosted grass.
Beyond the wire fence the silver birches
Stand erect, slender trunks spotted black
The filigree branches motionless in the cold morning air.

Bay Park, scarcely hidden by the trees
Is dressed in silver lame,
The green underskirt peeking through as
The river, glistening and inviting
curves towards Derry
Like a glimpse of the ice maiden's thigh.

The twin spires like sentinels stand
As bells ring out on Christmas morning
Heralding the birth of a baby
The maiden city has been breached
By peace and goodwill towards all.

Madeline McCully, Derry

Madeline McCully said: "I have dabbled in writing for several years but have only recently begun to write poetry. I am a practicing artist who has exhibited worldwide. Several of my poems and short stories have already been published. Most of my work is rooted in Ireland in past and contemporary culture. I see poetry as painting a picture in words, I hope to include some of my poetry on the website. www.irishlandscapes.net."

A NOTE

This is just to say
That today, for a paralysing moment,
I felt your tragedy
And sat in your place
Overwhelmed by choking senses of grief.
And then they faded,
Diluted and dispersed,
And as my comfortable earth emerged again
To envelope me securely,
I knew I was glad
I wasn't you.
I writhe in shame.

Joy Bell, Belfast

Joy Bell said: "I was born in Belfast. I am married, with three daughters and five grandchildren. I teach English in a special school, where I enjoy producing the annual musical. My writing has mostly been in the form of articles and drama scripts. But I have recently discovered the freedom of expressing deep feelings in poetry, of which this is an example. The poets who influence me most are Emily Bronte and Seamus Heaney."

NEVER BE AFRAID TO CRY

Life takes its toll on everyone
Emotions build up within us so powerful
Stress hammers inside us seeing no way out
Tension builds into what seems like unclimbable mountains

Never be afraid to cry.....for tears are a release
They break down the stranglehold of stress and tension

Tears are a gift we are often afraid to use
Tears can melt the hardest heart
Tears can heal the deepest wounds

Never be afraid to cry.... for a good cry is often the best
medicine of all

Tears.....the healer within us all
We are stronger than we know
When needed....any day...or any time
Never be afraid to cry

Betty Devenney, Strabane, County Tyrone

LOOK TO THE STARS

When the hand of desperation
Seems to hold you tight
And your tears are cold and empty
Though they echo through the night
When the sea will part for others
But the gate is closed for you
Don't be ashamed to fight it
Love will pull you through

When your eyes are feeling tired
From all the tears you've cried
Reach for a star and hold it
Believe hope hasn't died
When all the promises made
Seem to fade and fall away
Try to see there's someone out there
Who'll stay true to what they say

Gemma Walker, Waterside, Londonderry

Born and brought up in Londonderry **Gemma Walker**
enjoys acting, writing and outdoor pursuits. "I started writ-
ing poetry when I was 11, because I was encouraged to
pursue my interest in creative writing," she explained.
"Poetry is an emotional outlet for me and my work is influ-
enced by my experiences. I would described my style as
honest. I can be brutal but I try to capture optimism in
everything. I would like to be remembered as a person who
brought a little light into the lives of those she loved." Aged
16 she is a student with an ambition to travel the world so
that she can expand her experiences, meet new people and
learn new things. She has written many poems and had
several published.

SUMMERTIME FUN

She runs to me her arms so wide
As she clambers off her slide
Full of smiles and hair a mess
She's made short work of that new dress
Splattered in mud from a nearby creek
When she spied a frog I heard her shriek.
Her hair was shiny clean and fresh
But now it's an untidy mess
Adorned with grass and bits of twigs
Her daisychain scatters as she jigs
A cardigan which was scarcely worn
Now both elbows have been torn
Climbing stealthily up a tree
A thrushes nest she was keen to see
Kids should be seen and not heard I'm told
But try telling that to my four year old.
Who screams and yells and whoops so loud
she often gathers quite a crowd
of people who have come to see
My little tomboy at play with me

Linda Callaghan, Waterside, Londonderry

*Dedicated to the late Ms Audrey Sweeney (03.03.36 - 03.06.95)
and her sister Jennifer, who instilled in me a love of words. Also to
my darling daughter Victoria.*

Linda Callaghan said: "I am an artist, specialising in hand-paint-
ing silk scarves. I am 40 years old, divorced and live in my home-
town with my daughter Victoria, aged 14 years. I worked in a chil-
dren's home for 15 years and was sad to leave it. My poems are
based on true life experiences and I believe that kindness, honesty
and humour are vital in life. This poem is my first printed work,
although I have written and performed in a short skit in our local
theatre - the event was recorded in our local papers, the
Londonderry Sentinel and the Derry Journal."

DEAR BUS CONDUCTOR

My friend Julie really fancies you
She wants you to get married
And get a house and some babies
And a loan from Credit Union for holidays
I think its silly - she doesn't even know your name
And I think you're as old as her daddy
She says, "Age doesn't matter when you love someone"
I say "It matters now cos he doesn't love you
If he did you'd get on the bus for free"

Aisling Doherty, Derry

MOONLIGHT

The Sun was all cloaked up in night,
Her face was turned to purest white,
It drifted on a sea of blue
Tinted with a velvet hue.
The lady, by the lake so clear,
Sighs a sigh and sheds a tear.
Her sadness flowing from her eyes;
She hangs her head, and softly cries.
The Moon, she sees her pale face
And covers her in silver lace.
But she, consumed by so much woe
Herself into the lake would throw.
She sighs a sigh and looks above,
To wish, someday, to find true love.
Stars watch the lady reminisce;
The Moon sends down an Angel's Kiss.
She sees the rain begin to play,
She turns; She sighs, and walks away.

Linda Smith, County Tyrone

SERENDIPITY

As far as I could see the esplanade was empty;
No one walking his dog, no joggers,
No boat on the sea; no plane in the air.
Bright sun, blue sky, ultramarine water.
There was I early one morning on the coastal path,
When - magical moment - I saw him
On the rocks. I stood still and watched.
A cormorant, scarce four feet away
Drying his wings in the sunshine.
He raised his head, shook the feathers,
Turned round, looked at me - did he see me?

We stayed like that, a tableau
On that bright May morning.
An arrested moment out of eternity.
I looked around to share this glory
But there was no one there at all,
Just the bird on the rock and an ageing woman.
Two of us in all the world.
I shall never forget him
And the happiness he gave me.

Beatrice M Wilson, County Down

BECOMING A TEENAGER

Speak to me child, what's troubling your mind?
I've time to listen, I am honest and kind.
I look in your eyes but I cannot see
You tell me you thoughts whatever they be.

We all have times when life gets us down
But someone cares, so wipe off that frown.
Becoming a teenager is a big change to us all
I know you'll come through it, and be strong and tall.

So let's sit together, and have a long talk
Or maybe go out for a nice relaxing walk.
Where we can examine that pretty little head
And all of your worries, I hope I can shed.

Family and love, some children don't have
You have it all, there's no need to be sad.
Come into my arms, and let's have a cuddle
Together we can work out, this strange teenage muddle.

Elaine Warren French, County Antrim

THE LONELY PLACE

I came onto this lonely place,
So peaceful and serene,
No earthly hand had fashioned here,
Mother nature reigned supreme.

Through dappled shade and leafy glade,
The mind can wander free,
Wildflowers and trees, the rustling breeze,
In nature's harmony.

The soft tinkle of a little stream,
In a hidden place below,
As it winds its way through mossy dell,
Where the ferns and willows grow.

In such a place, with time and space,
Life's problems cease to be,
The sweet solitude of this lonely wood,
And its quiet sanctuary.

Then suddenly, a wild, raucous cry,
As a startled bird seeks open sky,
The magic spell is broken now,
I breathe a little sigh.

John V McManus, Larne, County Antrim

JOCK

I met this homely man from the Isle of Skye,
His name was Jock O'Donnell
And just for him I'd die.

He cuddled up to me one night
And asked for a kiss
And when I opened my mouth
He got an awful whiff.

I wondered what the problem was
But he wouldn't tell me then
So I lit another cigarette and stubbed it out again.

So after three more nights with him
He turned to me and said
You are such a bonnie lass so I've got to tell you then.
You know your teeth they need a scrub
(God I almost died)
I'm terrified of dentists, and I told him so
He said to me oh Maggie it's not so bad you know
So I'm at the dentist, and I want to let you know
Jock he may be leaving me or my teeth might have to go.

Caroline Morton, Lisburn

PAGES

Turn the page,
But it's the same book.
It's a little older, more space taken up,
But it's the same book.

Turn the page,
Back to the same sheet.
It's a little further away, not as close,
But it's the same page.

Tear the page,
It still has left its mark.
The writing is gone, a lack of words,
But the message remains.

Simon Maltman, Bangor

WEDDING DAY AT ST PAULS, RAMSEY

Bells ring out over town and sea,
While guests await the bride to be
Smiling faces greet each other
Father, mother, sister, brother.
To face the future without fears
For it's Susan's wedding year.
Oh happy day, "Here comes the bride"
The bridegroom patiently waits inside
Heads turn, "Will Susan smile?"
Nerves forgotten for a while.
Promises made, exchange rings,
The organ plays, and people sing
Drive through villages and country roads.
To Glen Helen, the reception, speeches and toasts.

Nancy Callow, Ramsey, Isle Of Man

J.B.

What was once clean and pure
Can soon become so black and blue
Covered with indentations
Underlined with dashes of red
Scored and marked through intelligence
Right or wrong, we've made our statement
How we feel and what we think
It's all put down in ink.

Matthew Walker, Bangor, County Down

OBJECTS OF DESIRE

"Love you" he says, in present tense;
selfless, so she'll not object
to him, the subject of that sentence,
and she the prime object.

Somewhere in that web of words,
the hungry spider lies
in weaved spell of verbs;
want, and need and other lies.

Hunters must seek their prey,
while pilgrims search for grails;
to praise and to pray
and lock their loves in jails.

Where they don't see the bars,
just the spaces in between the stars.

Noel Lindsay, County Antrim

TREE-PRESENCE

Friend, mentor, soul-mate,
how I have needed and clung to your tı
to your profound earthing,
to your self-contained completeness,
to the upward and outward stretch of your sou
that branches out to frame the naked open sky.
I have swayed within your shelter,
I have laid my cold shaking hands flat against you,
I have leaned my back against the strong support of you.
At close of day, your tracery reveals to me
the golden dish of moon, inviting me to feast
upon her light.

Sometimes my autumn eyes, full of change and pain,
cannot see you as evergreen. Sometimes I stand alone
and rigid beneath the private canopy of my silent darkness,
unable to reach out.
How I yearn for the time when I may cease from wandering
the paths of emptiness,
and discover my own deep forest
within the wilderness of my lonely soul.

Shelley Tracey, County Antrim

LY

I tried to laugh
I tried to cry
But couldn't get it out
By hook or by crook
I read the book
Wondered why
Still left me in doubt

The things behind the sun
What's going on in your brain
What road do I take
In this life what have I done
Just a fool standing in the rain
I hear the thunder
And I start to quake

My days are speeding away
My nights go rolling by
This is the season when day becomes night
And night becomes day
this is the time of no reply.

Adrian McGinley, Dunmurry, Belfast

BEFORE

Attempt to succeed; fabled word therapy
Anxious; on-edge; disguising it well
Though all can tell.

Hopeful, fearful: fusion of both
Need to succeed, excuse the meander
Like a spurned love I crave all they teach
Patient; In wait for the stars yet to reach.

Optimistic throughout;
Lesson I would not be without
Fulfilment, regardless.

Julieann Campbell, County Derry

THE PROPOSAL

If I should love you, let there be laughter not tears
If you should love me, let me not count the years
If I should love you, let the stars sing your name
If you should love me, let our hearts know no pain
If I should love you, may your voice fill my ear
If you should love me, may our lives know no fear
If I should love you, let it not be in vain
If you should love me, let us both feel the same
If I should love you, may our love make me brave
If you should love me, may it grow and not fade
If I should love you, let me fill up your life
If you should love me, let me call you my wife

John Deehan, Waterside, Derry City

LONELINESS

Creeping behind the shadows all alone.
Wet tears trickling like a lost frightened child,
This deserts so barren, this jungles so wild,
I am trapped forever in a one man zone.
In this lonely silence I hear my stomach groan,
There's no escape from the silence of this night
Fear grips my heart. Am I just an unnatural clone?
I am falling so far beyond my control.
Someone catch me, save, help me, quickly.
Speak to me, be my comfort and my friend.
Let me no longer feel alone and sickly.
I feel your touch, closer my need to attend.
My restraint is gone. Contentment fills my soul.

Joanne Peden, Ballymoney, County Antrim

THE TIDES OF HOPE

Floating in a sea of opportunity
There are chances
There are chancers
There are people likely to succeed

Absorbed in the game
There are players
There are cheats
There are people born lucky

Lost in a world of adventure
There are travellers
There are free loaders
There are people flying free

In the sea of life's opportunity
Play the game
Experience the adventure
Die a good death

Marlene McKenzie, Ballyclare, County Antrim

TRADITIONS

Throughout this city you will find
Beneath this northern sky
A people divided by traditions
Those like you and I
No attempt made to reconcile
Nor even the thought to try
This city surrounded by famous walls
Remains a city divided between
Those loyal to the British crown
Against those with an all Ireland dream
many unashamed in using God's name
Demanding rights for the orange or green
Is there a friendly hand to reach out
To break traditions, will someone dare
To show the people like you and I
The life we all could share
What no eyes have ever seen
Nor ears have ever heard.

Pearse Coyle, Derry City, County Derry

THE CAUSEWAY

I sit on the edge of existence, the wind so strong in my face
I find it hard to catch my breath.
As the waves crash into the rocks beneath me the spray
reaches
my skin and awakens me.
I sit facing the future, bleak, cold and uninviting.
I turn to see what has brought me this far.
A pathway of trials and decisions.
I sit on the edge of existence not knowing what the future
will hold, but knowing it is not in my hands.

Suzanne McCrory, Lisburn, County Antrim

THE FIELD

In the corner,
Of a field,
It sits
Cold and decrepit,
With no-one near,
Once was a house,
With voices heard,
A motorbike, sat at the door,
A river ran through,
And by the tree, at the corner,
A caravan, where we lived,
When I was born.

Damian Begley, Strathfoyle, County Derry

MOTHER

Cruelly robbed of your life at thirty seven years,
your departure created havoc and tears.
So very sad that your body had worn,
before you could grow with the children you had borne.
What must have been going through your mind
when told of your illness so unkind?
Great sadness is what we feel because you have been taken
and sometimes we pinch ourselves to awaken,
from the numbness and loneliness, our companions each
day
and from depreciating thoughts that won't go away.
They say that time will heal our wounds,
that we cannot believe as yet another day looms.
Kind words have been spoken, but they are just a token,
for nothing can replace the bonds that have been forever
broken.
No-one can answer our question why
that cruel illness overpowered your body and made you
slowly die.
We pray that God wraps you in his loving arms
free from pain, suffering and all that harms.

Louise McMonagle, Culmore, Derry City

Dedicated to my Mother Philomena McMonagle whose self-lessness remains indelibly and lovingly remembered by all of her nine children.

A SMILE

It can brighten a heart on
the dreariest day,
It can banish a worry a mile away.
It can make a lonely person
feel happy and gay.
That's what a smile can do.

It can help ease the the burden of
a sorrowing soul,
It can delight little children
as we past them stroll.
It can comfort the sick,
make a broken heart whole,
Yes, a smile helps to do
all that too.

So smile all you can, while
you've got the chance,
Smile as you go, with a
friendly glance.
It will brighten your outlook,
your whole life enhance,
So do try to smile, won't
you?

Sheila Jameson, Belfast

THAT SUNNY DAY

The sun was shining that day
We picked flowers, as we talked
I felt so safe, because your strong hand held mine
That memory will forever in my heart be locked.

The small village where we lived
Held lots of young folk
My friends, I'd say were plenty
I can still see you there, watching over me
Back then, my young heart couldn't possibly
Feel empty.

At such a young age, I still realised
I held a special place in your heart
You had lots of grandchildren and loved them all
But you and I, we were rarely apart.

You're no longer with me, this I know
But I see you in each sunny day
You see, I knew back then, as we picked the flowers
That the memory would forever with me stay.

Sadie Higgins, Ballyclare, County Antrim

*I dedicate this poem to my late Grandmother Martha Simms,
who had a big influence on all our lives.*

WHAT IS FRIENDSHIP?

A friend is someone who is always there,
holding you up through times of despair,
a friend to you as you are to me,
never at any cost or fee.

Sharing the hugs and laughter along the
years, wiping away each others tears,
building a lifetime of memories and much, much
more, both holding the key to the open door.

You've touched my heart, we've grown together,
there is no distance between us.
In each other we can depend
you are my life my treasured friend.

Lynne Morrow, Dungannon, County Tyrone

*I dedicate this poem to Shirley Hayes. We have been best
friends over a decade. Thank you Shirley for your friendship.*

DOLPHINS SONG

Deep blue sea
Sunshine shining blue.
Deep in the ocean
The dolphins sounds are heard,
Squawks, whistles, burps and clicks,
They sing their songs of love,
Rising up out of the ocean,
Like fireworks in the sky,
They leap so gracefully into the air,
And dive back in again,
Oh what lovely mammals,
The dolphins really are,
They reach out to us,
With their hearts,
And try to make us understand,
That the world can be so beautiful,
If we only take the time,
To have a look around us,
And look with our hearts and minds.

EM Gillen, Ballymena, County Antrim

Dedicated to two very special people, for all their continuing love and support. My Mum and Dad. Love E. X

THE ANNIVERSARY

Back in 1965
A bloody marriage was made and it survived
There were ups and downs, and even fights
Sometimes we were a sorry sight
And then six of the best came into our lives
In the early days it was trouble and strife
We watched them grow and make their way
Can you believe it's 35 years to the day
We've slowed down a a bit
But we're still able
To me you're the tops and I still look like Betty Grable
I've no regrets, things can only get better
As long as we stick it out together
It must have been love, it's lasted so long
Yes, 35 years and still going strong.

M A McCafferty, Newtown Abbey, Belfast

ANTRIM

Travelling in a thousand places,
but in my heart you still strike a chime.
In every street old familiar faces,
as if enchantment, takes part of time.

Nature never fixed a golden vision more enticing,
while moving in a curvaceous, lush way.
Sprinkling my childhood cake with snow capped icing,
as pure silver in wishes is given to Lough Neagh.

Victor Shaw, County Antrim

BUCKTON CASTLE

Buckton Castle, A ring-like Neolithic mound
stands high, stop a dark Pennine hill,
Power and domination radiate, still
from the crest of this louring pile.

A quarry eats insidiously, Rodent-like
into the hard rock which lies beneath.
Destructive dynamite, blast endlessly
at the roots of this ancient chiefs' abode.

Rise, old warrior, rise, old priest.
And quell the hungry bulldozers roar, strike
down the man who rapes the past for cash,
Hurl his corpse upon the share traders floor.

Alan Lawton, Douglas, Isle Of Man

ODE TO LIFE

Now it's the year 2001
and it feels like life has
just begun.
I feel so better and happier inside
no more need to cover,
No more need to hide.

I'm excited about the days ahead,
A big change from wanting to stay in bed.
Everyday brings something new,
That me and him, can get up and do.

It feels so good to be a part
of someone else's loving heart.
The closeness that I feel for him,
Has opened my heart up deep within.

Patricia O'Reilly, Belfast

UNQUENCHABLE THIRST

"Time for last drinks"
The hedonist's heart sinks.
Even though they have had enough
Of that fiery liquid, the devil's stuff.

They crave for more
In the hope that their mood will soar,
Until they think it is the taste of paradise
this whiskey and ice.

Morning falls with the barbarity of the executioners axe.
Crawl beneath the covers and hide, no time to relax
until the next bout of sensual and mental drowning takes place,
To wash away inhibitions then integrity, leaving you empty and in disgrace.

Aaron Donaghy, Banbridge, County Down

PAST

Stand alone and try to forget about the past,
Let the truth in your heart abide,
Think of the future and not what happened last.
Remember that the world is wide.
Do not let the loneliness rule your mind
The future is in your hands.
Do not forget that there is a better love to find.
So many places still to land.

A heart is worth more once it has been broken,
You deserve more than simple love tokens.
Throw it back in his face,
Tell him you want more.
Your life will not go to waste
and your heart cannot be tore.

Colette Timoney, Strabane, County Tyrone

THE AWAKENING

The piercing shrill of an alarm clock, slices the silence of
morning air
and its power is such that it gives such a scare
It if it does not switch off soon, that clock is sure to greet
its doom.

Aroma of strong caffeine, to awaken the spirits of the dead
Other bodies begin to rise, all wearing their morning guise
Like zombies arising from their tombs, each leave their
room.

The first brave soul to utter a word receives responses not
quite humane
The bodies of the souls begin to awaken under strain
And so it leaves to ponder if only mornings could come
much later
Then perhaps the rising would less feel like
the awakening of the dead.

Maeve Cairns, Lurgan, County Armagh

THE TREE

Higher and higher the tree it does grow
Waving its branches to and fro
Stretching to reach the heat from the sun.
Patiently waiting for spring time to come.

The leaves they appear like a tight little curl
Ever so slowly they start to unfurl
The tree in its splendour a glorious sight
Welcoming birds from their long winter flight

All through the summer in its mantle of green
The birds build their nests they chatter and preen
The branches they move with a slow gentle sway
Supremely it stands in its wondrous array.

The autumn will come, the birds fly away
Through the leaves on the ground the children will play
The tree stands there proudly, its roots in the soil
Gathering strength for another year's toil.

A Belshaw, Bangor

THE EMPTY CHAIR

Life it's just a game
But whenever we lose we look for someone to blame
I lie awake while I sleep
Wondering when this game will be complete
I stand, I sit, I lean up straight
And go to bed early while I stay up late
I'm no-one special, not one of a kind
And why I'm here, I search for a sign
But this is my life and it's ending one minute at a time
I sit in a crowded room alone
Talk to no-one on my phone
Have a discussion all by myself
Have no photographs upon my shelf
I'm just drifting by from day to day
Life is a game but I don't want to play
Going to give the dice a final throw
If it's not even then I think I'll go
Because I feel like a riddle, to which the answer no-one
knows
I feel like sunshine when people expect snow
I feel like the guy at the back of the line
I feel like rain in the summertime
If I was gone would anyone care
Would anyone notice the empty chair

John Coups, Strabane, County Tyrone

LONGWAVE RADIO

A restless sea, undulating through time and space,
Frenzied waves crashing on acoustic shores.
Soft, overlapping ripples without connecting wires,
Messages in a gentle cascade.

Each oscillation a crest or trough
Of souls enchantment or hearts despair,
Sinuously sweeping our dreams along
To an undiscovered melancholy.

Victor McMullen, Lurgan, County Armagh

HUGS

A hug is a simple thing to give,
It's one of our human needs.
Each generation are given hugs,
Hence hugs are like planted seeds.

Words are needless when you give hugs,
It's a quiet understanding.
Hugs vanquish agitation,
Then people are less demanding.

Doubts diminish when you are hugged,
All feel the closeness of love.
It's wonderful this warm embrace,
The inventor was God above.

Louise Gibson, Ballymena, County Antrim

SPRING

Winter passes, and as spring draws near
The days become brighter
And the climate becomes hotter,
as summer draws near.

The clocks are moved an hour forward
and the days become longer.
Flowers start to blossom
as the weather gets warmer.

Spring is when you wake up
to the birds singing in the trees.
To a beautiful morning
and a long day.

Edel Jordan, Benburb, Dungannon, County Tyrone

TO A SPECIAL FRIEND

There's always something
To look forward to
A special occasion nice things to do
Or one yet to meet
A dream to be realised
Someone to greet
A little surprise to brighten your day
Or perhaps loving words
That someone will say
Keep looking forward
Enjoy all the fun
And try to remember
The best friend, yet to come

Wilma Lewsley, Lurgan, County Armagh

MY LITTLE HANDS BELONG TO ME

I have two little thumbs you know, they follow me
everywhere I go,
and oh, dear me I love them so, where would I be without
them.

They help me button up you see, and they only
belong to dear little me, they're always right here
close by me, so where would I be without them.

They have little brothers and sisters four, and on
my other hand they have four more, to help me
open up a door and help me do a big lot more.

There my own little tiny hands you see and I
tell you this they belong to me and if I hadn't got
them close by me, where would I be without them.

Mrs M Smith, Glengormley

MIDNIGHT SWIMMER

I can see you clearly even now
Surging porpoise-backed through silver tracery,
Deaf to dire parental woes
Of jagged rocks and undertows.

The moon anoints you, sea child,
Child and votive you dissolve,
Folding inwards, voluptuous,
Yielding to the creeping tide.

But I stand still, as then,
A stiff-legged sentinel,
Half in wonder, half in envy,
And sadly certain you will not beckon me
Into your watery raptures.

Hugh Harley, Londonderry

THE ASCENT OF MAN

In space.
On the Moon.
In the air.
On the land.
Under the sea.
On Television.
In books.
In the food.
In heads.
From mouths.

Robert Gillespie, Londonderry

LOVE

Love is a word I can't explain
Love takes us on a journey to another plane
Love gives new hope when it is found
By living life on solid ground

Love I see in twinkling eyes
Love I feel in heart-felt surprise
Love it calms my troubled mind
Peace returns, gentle, kind

Love lifts me high when I feel low
Even through the winter snow
Love warms my soul, keeps me alive
Lifts my heart, wondrous surprise

Mrs R Dornan, Ballyclare, County Antrim

WINTER QUEEN

You're the *winter queen*
Icy cold and shouldn't be seen
They all reach out to you
But to the south your warmth has flew

You're like shattered glass
Can't let the good things last
They all end up with wounds
Left to roam barren moons

You're like a November wind
Pass judgement on those who have sinned
They all end craving absolution
You tease them with formulas without giving solutions

You charm them in with enchantment
Make them feast off your chocolate apartment
Then you close your doors, banish the light
Leave them in limbo unable to fight

Brigidette McAnea, Drumquin, County Tyrone

WONDER YEARS

You walk through life full of wonder
replaying your mistakes and blunders
Sometimes the sky shines so bright
Other times grey billow cease the light
We'll laugh at joys that pass us by
everyday we try

Try in life to make it what we want
we need to live our life we must succeed
we pass right through the years slip on
Childhood teenage years all have gone
and then we're old and reminiscing
and wonder of things we might have been missing
grey billow are coming to cease my light
when I pass on again the sky shines bright
I've lived and lost my wonder years

Lisa Doherty, Waterside, County Derry

*I'm dedicating this to Paul, Shannon, Chelsea, Kellie-ann,
Mum, Dad, my four brothers, and Auntie Trina xxx. Love you
all.*

FAITH

A delicate gift
Sometimes consolidated sometimes challenged
Even sometimes mocked
By the heavy presence of Experience

Experience versus Faith
An intense conflict which can't be missed
Experience throws a punch at Faith
But will Faith be subverted?

Faith rises to its feet
But Experience towers over it
And Faith falls to its knees
Has Faith lost its strength?

We can watch this fight passively?
We can turn off this commentary on the
television or radio?
We can become involved in this conflict and make a differ-
ence?
Justice always prevails?

Lucinda McCloskey, Limavady, County Derry

SINEADS WEDDING

We are gathered here in the chapel today
to celebrate the joining of two people in a special way.
In love and loyalty, to cherish each other for ever
that they will always be together.
May God bless them all their lives,
And all other husbands and wives.
We hope their relationship will grow in love and care
married now they are a pair.
This day is both happy and sad,
But everyone is glad,
Sinead and Kieran have received another sacrament,
That the holy spirit has gracefully sent.
They will remember this day for ever more
to their new life this marriage opens the door.
I wish them the very best,
And I'm sure so does every guest.
As family another sister of mine has left.
The last thing to be said,
Is that they are now happily wed.

Nuala McKay, Randalstown, County Antrim

ENDINGS

Caught by the scruff of my own politeness,
too weak once more to walk away,
I bear, through fumes of aftershave,
the battering from this endless bore.
Puffed pigeon proud of his power of mind,
innocent of triteness,
he holds the floor;
a wink of gold watch marks another wave:
"It seems to me, in my opinion, I,
Take for example me, personally speaking, my..."
Meanings blur, nerve ends grind.
What can a victim do or say;
Hopeful of their random rightness
I loose the fitful nod, the aimless yes,
for every story ends with his success.

It's painful even now to tell
of one who talked upon me as a friend.
His story finally reached its routine end,
and I remember very well
not going to his funeral.

Noel Spence, Comber, County Down

144

LOVE

Love is like a song
It demands to be heard
It happens so suddenly
And cannot be learned

It has it's own sound
Unlike anything else
You can't close the door
Or put it on a shelf

It comes right through
And reaches for your heart
But love isn't all good
For it tears couples apart

It can be like a deadly rose
With thorns that will pierce
It can be so painful and it
Can be so fierce

The sun may rise
And the moon may set
But the love you lost
You will never forget

Natalie Dunn, Shantallow, Derry

SPRING

Spring comes reluctant to these northern shores
But winter cannot fight the sharp spears
Of daffodils and snowdrops in his path.
He retreats vanquished while the cold tears
Of melting frost rain down upon the grass

I have long waited for this happy day
When looking out across the orchard bare
A faint green film appears above the trees
The tiny leaves unfolding under there
Tomorrow a pink border will decorate the green

The brook escapes its icy prison, rendering to lace
The ice that bound it through each winter day
A sudden breeze disturbs the brown leaves
Surprised to find them free once more to play
Winter has long held them to her breast

The busy sparrows rustle in the ivy wall
Each searching for his own secluded place
The blackbird struts his stuff upon the fence
Challenging all comers, "This is my space"
While his mate quietly sits upon the nest

Norah Burnett, Richhill, County Armagh

LOVE

Love is like a river, forever flowing
Love is like a child, forever growing
Love is like a hole, digging deep
Love can be painful, hard to keep

Love resembles the sun, burning bright
Love resembles the moon, shining its light
Love resembles the stars, away up high
Love can be a death, it too can die

Love has its ups, happy and joyful
Love has its downs, sad and sorrowful
Love is a gift from me to you
Love is there whatever you do

Love is for the rich, as strong as gold
Love is for the poor, as weak as mold
Love is for all, you and me
Love is powerful, reach out and see

Clare Rainey, Derry City

BIG ANTON

When I remember you granda,
I'll see your crooked smile,
recall quirky sense of humour,
everlasting pipe,
spent matches scattered in grate
or replaced discretely in Swan box
to cohabit with the living.
I'll remember stories told
of exile from your beloved Derry.
Tales of country schoolrooms;
turf-fires fed by sods that children
carried, anxious to please.
The skin on lukewarm milk
thawed out on icy mornings.
Dry toilets; clocks; rats; mice;
woodworm; ceilings that sagged
and roofs that leaked....
your pride in a job well done, alphabet of pupils success.
These I'll remember, granda,
Big Anton, truly a big, big man.

Tessa Johnston, County Derry

148

OF THE SEA

A streak of silver on each crest,
Of each ripple in an inky black gloss.
A gentle sloshing as the water of all directions
Creeps onto the shore,
A never-ending stretch of midnight bruise, eerily still and
cold,
Not wanting to share the mysteries and secrets it holds.
Then, a glowing red sun and sweet
Chirping of children,
Illuminate a deep romantic blue,
Hot and gentle, so innocently lying and laughing,
Lazily drifting, pretending not of its night-time sentiment.

Jemma Robinson, Dungannon, County Tyrone

THE AVOCET

Ireland's glossary of peaceful terms,
Whether it be permissive attitudes or
Love-thy-neighbour, were slumping in supply.
The avocet, wading through the ripples of
Lets-pretend-peace and guarantees,
Decided not to simply allow hope to subside:
Letting its bill come into the process,
It said, "Each man should be a teetotaller,
As if drink and war were of the same genus."

Colin Dardis, Cookstown

DERRY CITY

With bayonet poised the savage sailor thrusts
Above forgot remembered names,
Astride the green streaked concrete pedestal
Of bronze leaked verdigris.

Diamond, the rounded square and centrepoint
Encircled by the grey arrogance,
Of buildings fronted with elaborate stone
And one roof of green malachite.

Shadow shaded streets of sundry shops
Sinew out in four directions,
Stretched and finalised with arch topped gates
Shipquay, Ferryquay, Butcher, Bishop.

The wide walled city snugly sits
Unprotected, impotent cannon facing out,
While open ghostly unseen gates permit the entry
Of the brash and unhindered world.

Guildhall, red sentry figure and four clock-faced
Donging the daylight hour with monotone,
Stiffly guards the wide two bridged river Foyle
One streamlined high above, the craggy lord below.

John F McCartney, Eglinton, County Derry

CONTINUUM

Scarred into my maternal hood
From the stars above
like my sisters before me
You are with me since my own conception.

I carried you all through my childhood,
nurturing myself in readiness for you.

Now I have passed onto you
The precious seeds of us
It is your turn to enjoy your time as yourself
Before you too join the continuum.

Patricia Millar, Hollywood, County Down

SEPTEMBER CHILD

September Child you are the one
Who so loved life, September Child
You fried so hard just to survive
Yet you were hurt by a cruel disease
Leukaemia - a dark cloud touched your life
Yet you stayed strong for you family
For your friends and all your loved ones
You are the rain that cleansed my tears
You will always be my September Child
When I see your face, your radiant smile
Your deep blue eyes, your chestnut hair
I think of you.
Through your bravery others have survived
You will always be my September Child
Such love goes on forever more
To eternity, *Karen Lesley*, my September Child.

Maureen J Archbold, Larbert

THE STORM

The clouds have approached in the dulling sky,
The droplets of rain are falling from high.

A chill has emerged in the atmosphere.
Distant rumbles of thunder, occur in my ear.

The whistling wind shrieks like a banshee,
As it circulates through the trembling trees.

Shivers creep up the animals' spines,
As they search for shelter beneath the pines.

The tension is growing, becoming fate,
Lightening is present, not a minute late.

Shudders in roof-tops, a flickering light.
The storm has arrived, and it's here for the night.

Cathy Kelly, Ballymena, County Antrim

CREATION MEETS CREATION

The trees of the field will clap their hands
and the wind will rush to meet you
The birds will give you feathers to wear
and the light will surround and heal you
The sun will rise for you alone
on the part of the earth where you stand
Your eyes will see what they never saw
and in so doing your vision will expand
In peace and joy
Open hearted to beauty
You'll abandon your soul to the living land
and creation will rejoice in your being

Jean Gardner, Belfast

MYOPIC

This forest's lens
Unfurls a fish eyed view,

Of the hieroglyph fowl prints
As they artfully dance to the thaw.

So remember the oak bole
As you pass,
And curtsy the holly berries,
Hushed meeting.

Wolf and Red Riding Hood,
Asleep, under the

Vast, blank foolscap
Of sky.

Derek Keilty, Belfast

TOM'S POEM

Dear God, protect my son, a child
Against a world both hard and wild.
Shield my little lad from sin,
I hope his battle he will win;
That fight, at such enormous cost,
In pain I fear his father lost.
Dear Christ, I wanted to stay longer;
But while I have to keep away,
I dream of Tom and pray each day.

Ivan Walton, Londonderry

ON THE WAVES

Misty hills guard the evening sky
as the white bird dips and flutters
on the dark waters.
Beacons of red and gold welcome safely
to the harbour.
She moves gracefully leaving strands of feathery foam
in the trailing wake
Passengers bid farewell
As she sighs in berth.

Hazel Wilson, Dundonald